Glenn Porter
Hagley Museum and Library

The Rise of Big Business

1860–1920

SECOND EDITION

Harlan Davidson, Inc.
Wheeling, Illinois 60090-6000

Library of Congress Cataloging-in-Publication Data

Porter, Glenn
    The rise of big business, 1860–1920 / Glenn Porter.—2nd ed..
        p. cm.—(The American history series)
    Includes bibliographical references and index.
    ISBN 0-88295-882-8
    1. Big business–United States—History. I. Title. II. Series: American his-
tory series (Wheeling, Ill.)
HD2356.U5P67   1992
338.6'44'0973–dc20   91-16506
                                                                CIP

Cover photograph: The Larkin Company Building, courtesy of The Larkin
Collection, Buffalo and Erie County Historical Society.

Book design: Roger Eggers

Manufactured in the United States of America
98 MG 6

FOREWORD

Every generation writes its own history for the reason that it sees the past in the foreshortened perspective of its own experience. This has surely been true of the writing of American history. The practical aim of our historiography is to give us a more informed sense of where we are going by helping us understand the road we took in getting where we are. As the nature and dimensions of American life are changing, so too are the themes of our historical writing. Today's scholars are hard at work reconsidering every major aspect of the nation's past: its politics, diplomacy, economy, society, recreation, mores and values, as well as status, ethnic, race, sexual, and family relations. The lists of series titles that appear at the back of this book will show at once that our historians are ever broadening the range of their studies.

The aim of this series is to offer our readers a survey of what today's historians are saying about the central themes and aspects of the American past. To do this, we have invited to write for the series scholars who have made notable contributions to the respective fields in which they are working. Drawing on primary and secondary materials, each volume presents a factual and narrative account of its particular subject, one that affords readers a basis for perceiving its larger dimensions and importance. Conscious that readers respond to the closeness and immediacy of a subject, each of our authors seeks to restore the past as an actual present, to revive it as a living reality. The individuals and groups who figure in the pages of our books appear as real people who once were looking for survival and fulfillment. Aware that historical subjects are often matters of controversy, our authors present their own findings and conclusions. Each volume closes with an extensive critical essay on the writings of the major authorities on its particular theme.

The books in this series are designed for use in both basic and advanced courses in American history, on the undergraduate and graduate levels. Such a series has a particular value these days, when the format of American history courses is being altered to accommodate a greater diversity of reading materials. The series offers a number of distinct advantages. It extends the dimensions of regular course work. Going well beyond the confines of the textbook, it makes clear that the study of our past is, more than the student might otherwise understand, at once complex, profound, and absorbing. It presents that past as a subject of continuing interest and fresh investigation. The work of experts in their respective fields, the series, moreover, puts at the disposal of the reader the rich findings of historical inquiry. It invites the reader to join, in major fields of research, those who are pondering anew the central themes and aspects of our past. And it reminds the reader that in each successive generation of the ever-changing American adventure, men and women and children were attempting, as we are now, to live their lives and to make their way.

John Hope Franklin
A. S. Eisenstadt

CONTENTS

PREFACE TO THE
SECOND EDITION

Almost twenty years have elapsed since the first edition of this book appeared. The passage of time and the accumulation of much new scholarship have caused me to recast much of the text, particularly the third chapter and the bibliographical essay. My views about the fundamental characteristics of big business and the basic forces that called it into being, however, have remained substantially as they were. But there has been important new work on the critical decade following the Panic of 1893, and on the ties between the emerging modern corporation and many other institutions in American life, especially science and technology, labor, and the university, as well as fresh studies on the creation of a white-collar workforce, on the nature of work, the role of women in the workplace, and the impact of the corporate way of life on the heartland. Further, rich new investigations of the perennial topic of the regulation of business have appeared. These new perspectives have led me to expand the treatment of the impact of the rise of big business beyond the narrowly political sphere in which historians for so long saw the major cultural and social meaning of the coming of the giant corporation. Since many of these broader social consequences were coming into focus in the decade before 1920, it seemed appropriate to extend the ter-

minal date for the period covered in the book. All such per-
iodizations are, as historians never tire of telling the world,
somewhat arbitrary and are not meant to be taken literally.

Along with the advance of scholarship, the historical
events of our own time have also played a part in shaping how
we think about big business and our past. (As historians also
never tire of saying, such considerations should not influence
our interpretations of more distant days, but they do.) For
example, it is clear that Americans are less fearful of business
than we were twenty years ago, although concerns over the
environmental consequences of unbridled growth and industrialization around the globe continue to haunt us and to cloud
what otherwise is largely an era of political acceptance of the
corporation. The continuing decline of labor unions and of
the left in domestic politics have served to reduce the vitality
and influence of many of the traditional critics of the corporation. Ironically, many large firms have at the same time
moved toward more responsible and politically shrewder positions on issues affecting global ecosystems, as well as other
political conflicts. As it has done since its earliest days, big
business has shown itself able to adapt to changing political
and social currents.

If we fear business less, many in the United States have
also come almost to fear for business. That is, American enterprise now seems less omnipotent, weaker than it did in the
era in which it set the pace for the spread of corporate power
around the industrial world. This may have made us less inclined to be critical of big business in its historical heyday.
The global success of giant corporations from other nations
makes American business appear less distinctive and probably
less dominant. Chronic national problems with the balance of
trade, a growing dependence on foreign lenders, and an inability to control government budgets perhaps play their parts
in subtly encouraging us to see the days of Standard Oil and
U.S. Steel as not so bad after all.

The decline of capitalism's great ideological foe has similarly had its effects. The widespread embracing of market sys-

tems and of corporate ways of managing economic activity
has served to remind us that big business has proven to be an
effective organizational form for meeting the perceived needs
of many nations, not just our own. Along with the globalization
of markets and the relative decline of American business on
the international stage, this has underscored the fact that big
business arose throughout much of the industrial world. It was
far more than just an American phenomenon. We now are
more likely to see the rise of large-scale enterprise in the United
States in that wider context than was the case earlier.

From many vantage points, the rise of big business now
seems more important in America's history than ever before.
It was the dominant institution of the twentieth century, reshaping much of society in its image and for its purposes. It
has proven to be the most effective instrument through which
we—and many others around the globe—have been able to
pursue the things that are most important to us in our material
civilization. Whether that has been for good or ill for the fate
of humankind on the planet is for each reader to determine.
What is beyond doubt is that the rise of big business was central
to the transformation of life in America for more than a century. I hope that this book may contribute to a better understanding of the structure and function of the modern corporation, how and why it arose and spread, and some of the ways
in which it had such a revolutionary impact on the world.

Finally, I want to close with a brief word of thanks to all
those who have played a role in this modest publication. Those
who have read it and commented upon it and offered helpful
suggestions are too numerous to list, as of course are those
whose scholarship undergirds the interpretive framework of
the book. Two particular scholars, however, must be acknowl-
edged. One is the man whose lifelong devotion to the history
of modern business enterprise has given shape and clarity to
the modern world's understanding of its most influential institution, and that is Alfred D. Chandler, Jr. His work has
revolutionized the study of business history, and it was my
good fortune to be his student many years ago. It has been my

privilege to be his colleague and friend ever since. The other is Louis Galambos. His scholarship and his gifted teaching have allowed him to attract and train many of the leading historians in the history of business. He taught me American history when I was a freshman in college, and he persuaded me that history was a good thing to do with one's life. I have always been grateful for those two teachers and scholars. Although they will certainly not agree with everything in this little book, they have taught the world much of what it knows of big business.

Glenn Porter
Hagley Museum and Library

CHAPTER ONE

What is Big Business?

The purpose of this volume is to impart some information and ideas about one of the most important, yet widely mis-understood, topics in American history—the coming of big business. Many of us have a limited understanding of our society, its government, and its past, but above all, of its econ-omy. This is not entirely our fault. Anyone who has watched economists trade jargon and conflicting predictions may feel that they are little more than soothsayers just back from ex-amining entrails. As for the general public, most Americans now clearly consider the existence of big business a normal and natural part of their lives, like the certainty of taxes and the four seasons. Many citizens, of course, continue to be deeply concerned about abuses of power by large corporations, the uncertain environmental effects of unbridled growth, and the dangers posed by the often intimate connections between business and government. Nevertheless, it is clear that the American political process has accepted the fact of the exist-ence of big business, that large-scale enterprises are hardly likely to be destroyed or fundamentally altered via political action, though their behavior will continue to be constrained and influenced by political and social criticisms. This acceptance was not always so clear.

Throughout our national history, Americans have shaped much of their politics around one or another variant of the struggle against big business. The lineage of ideas about the evils of large-scale business goes back at least as far as Thomas Jefferson. Later, Andrew Jackson and his followers molded an era around the fight to destroy the "monster" Bank of the United States and its influence. Both the populist and progressive movements, though extremely complex, were ultimately rooted in a deep reluctance to accept the rise of big business without protest. After an apparent national accommodation with the new economic order in the 1920s, the New Deal era witnessed what may well have been the Indian Summer of any genuine widespread interest in antitrust movements. The more recent rekindling of public interest in the shortcomings of big business, sparked by growing concerns about the environment and by critics such as Ralph Nader, may lead to significant change, though that remains to be seen. As America's competitive position in the world economy declined near the end of the twentieth century, criticisms also surfaced about the economic performance of the nation's businesses.

Most of our earlier political conflicts about business, like other political clashes, were couched in very vague terms. Few people were specific about what they meant by big business or how to correct its alleged evils. In addition, the opposition to large-scale business often was mixed with a confused array of related but distinct ideas such as the persistent idealization of rural, agrarian civilization—what Richard Hofstadter in *The Age of Reform* (1955) called the "agrarian myth." Most Americans of the late nineteenth and early twentieth centuries witnessed in confusion and doubt the passing of the older, agrarian society whose businesses were small, local affairs.

The coming of giant corporations was profoundly unsettling, for the process not only altered the way of life of the great majority of people, but it seemed to call into question many of the ideas and values by which Americans had defined themselves and their nation. The cult of individualism, the belief in competition and in democracy, the belief that individuals could rise through their own efforts to wealth and power—all seemed threatened by the giant corporations whose influence came to be felt in virtually every city and town across the land. Of the many changes that have occurred in our history, few if any have made such a deep and lasting difference as the emergence of an industrial civilization and its characteristic institution, the large corporation. Until recent decades, however, historians had talked a great deal about the opposition to business but had provided relatively little in the way of thoughtful generalizations about the process by which big business actually arose.

To some extent, historical work on the coming of giant corporations has reflected the rather paradoxical way in which Americans have responded to large-scale enterprise itself. At the same time that the American people were upset about the rise of big business, they were also eagerly embracing it. No other country in the world made antitrust such a major political issue, and none has exhibited the long running tradition of institutionalized concern about big business that has marked the United States. Paradoxically, few if any nations have created so many giant firms so quickly and have extended the bureaucratization of their economic activities so far as the United States. Americans have always admired giant economic organizations while at the same time fearing them, and the treatment of the rise of big business by American historians has reflected these conflicting popular views.

For many years, most historical assessments of the rise of big business were either emotionally slanted attacks on the "robber barons" or else attempts to refute such interpretations by focusing on the positive aspects in the coming of large-scale enterprises (that is, such contributions as greater productive efficiency and expanded economic growth). The first group of historians usually coupled a "liberal" or "progressive" political preference with a view of history in which the rise of big business was seen as the inevitable result of capitalism's continuous tendency toward the concentration of capital and production into larger and larger units. "If society is founded on the idea that property belongs to the strongest," Henry Demarest Lloyd argued in *Wealth Against Commonwealth* (1894), "these will sooner or later get all the property, by bargains or by battles according to 'the spirit of the age.' " Some of the better contributions to the robber baron school of historiography, such as Matthew Josephson's *The Robber Barons* (1934), demonstrated an appreciation of the varieties and complexities of history by acknowledging the role of factors such as entrepreneurship, technology, and plain good luck in shaping the coming of big business. Rather than lingering upon explanations of the coming of big business, however, such historical works usually featured moral denunciations of the avarice and ruthlessness of big business leaders, questioning the appropriateness of the wealth and power that society conferred on a relative few. Invoking the American ideals of political and economic democracy, Josephson denounced the "new nobility" whose members "organize and exploit . . . farmers and workers into harmonious corps of producers . . . only in the name of an uncontrolled appetite for private profit."

The opposing interpretation of the period was, for many years, that the business giants had made positive contributions by bringing greater efficiency and organization to the economy. This approach came to be known as the "industrial statesmen" view. By looking at events from the perspective of the business giants, these historians naturally came to see history in terms that made virtually all business behavior seem reasonable, and even praiseworthy. Sometimes this process of revisionism all but turned the robber baron approach on its head, as in Julius Grodinsky's *Jay Gould* (1957) and Maury Klein's more recent *Life and Legend of Jay Gould* (1986). Matthew Josephson had called Gould (an unscrupulous railroad promoter and stock manipulator of the 1870s and 1880s) "Mephistopheles." Klein's portrait of Gould was highly positive, and Grodinsky believed that Gould's schemes "performed a service to society" by encouraging competition. One could choose a political preference, observe the era from the standpoint of the large businesses or "the public interest," and conclude whether Carnegie, Rockefeller, Duke, and the others were robber barons or industrial statesmen.

The historical treatment of the coming of big business was part of the larger, twentieth-century trend toward "progressive history." Liberal historians interpreted American history as a series of conflicts between the forces of good (fighting for greater democracy and a more nearly equal distribution of wealth) and the opposing forces of conservatism (fighting to maintain the status quo). This interpretive tradition was dominant in America at least until the latter 1950s. Dissenters (usually called "revisionists") merely had a different set of political views; they did not alter the prevailing view of history as a moral struggle.

Much of the historical work of more recent decades has seriously eroded the progressive view of history. The "consensus" historians of the 1950s and 1960s emphasized what they saw as the relatively narrow range of political and social disagreement in the American past, and they undermined the progressive historians by pointing out the uglier sides (such as anti-Semitism, racism, and nativism) of various reform movements. Thereafter the New Left historians broke completely with progressive history's admiration for the liberal reform movements, denouncing the reformers for failing to bring more fundamental changes. Gabriel Kolko's *The Triumph of Conservatism* (1963), for example, painted the progressive movement as an essentially conservative phenomenon heavily influenced by business. Since the 1970s American historians have found broad, unifying, interpretive structures much less attractive and have turned to a mosaic of topics generally described as social history. Rather than viewing America's industrial civilization as a whole, they have instead focused on such subdivisions of it as the history of women, racial and ethnic minorities, labor, science and technology, and business.

The decline of progressive history, and perhaps the spreading dissatisfaction with traditional American liberalism as an organizing social philosophy, sent historians looking for new ways of doing history. Some turned to quantification and sought through voting analyses, demographic data, and econometric models to produce a new history that would qualify as a truly scientific "social science." Others, drawing on sociology, organization theory, and (to a much lesser extent) economics, have attempted to analyze process and structure without passing explicit moral judgments on the individuals and institutions of the past. This kind of work has been particularly evident in business history. The scholarship of Alfred D. Chandler, Jr., has come to dominate our understanding of the history of modern business, not only in the United States but throughout the developed world. In three major works, *Strategy and Structure* (1962), *The Visible Hand* (1977), and *Scale and Scope* (1990), Chandler demonstrated that the form and function of a business enterprise is shaped by the nature and complexity of the tasks it performs. Implicitly, this way of looking at history accepts the premise that the overriding, legitimate purpose of any business is to make a profit by employing resources productively over long periods of time. Further, it assumes that we can learn more about the history of business if we focus on understanding patterns of organizational structure and function than if we emphasize moral judgments about the motives of individuals.

This book is framed in that tradition. It looks at the rise of big business by examining the underlying institutional changes that made the large corporation possible, investigating the role of markets, changing transportation and communication networks, production processes, legal environments, financial institutions, and other factors. It also poses some questions about the wider implications of the new, giant businesses that rose to dominance in the American economy between the Civil War and World War I. By exploring these and similar questions, we may be able to reach a deeper understanding of this important part of American history than by approaching the topic seeking to assign blame or praise. Indeed, the rise of big business in time became a major theme in the history of virtually all industrial nations, regardless of their ideologies and cultures. America led the world into the age of big business and clearly set the economic pace globally until the decade of the 1970s. And, though business had always been a very strong influence in American society, since the rise of big business ours has been a culture strongly dominated by the values and mores of the corporation. Today it is difficult to imagine a world without large businesses, but the modern corporation was almost unknown in the United States of 1860. Within the course of only half a century or so, the American economy was transformed by the rise of big business. How did an institution that was barely present in the 1860s come to be the predominant economic form by the end of the second decade of the twentieth century? This book seeks to answer that question.

The essential first step is to be clear on what is meant by the term "big business." The purpose of this first chapter, therefore, is to provide a general definition of the nature and functions of big business; the creature will at least be surrounded if not completely subdued. It is important to understand the differences between this brand of large-scale enterprise and the smaller business firms common in America before the last half of the nineteenth century.

There are a great many kinds of businesses operating in the American economy. Major examples include: agriculture; forestry; mining; information processing; construction; transportation; communications; utilities; wholesale and retail trade; finance; service industries such as repair facilities and legal, medical, and educational businesses; and the operations of various governmental agencies. When Americans think of big business, however, they usually think of the large corporations engaged primarily in manufacturing—General Motors, IBM, Exxon, Du Pont, General Electric, and so on. (In recent decades they have also come to think of the many foreign-based giants that play a highly visible and growing role here—Toyota, Siemens, Sony, Mitsubishi, Michelin, BMW, and others.) In the era considered in this book, when people spoke of big businesses they usually had in mind three kinds of enterprises in particular: railroads, manufacturing companies, and banks. The individuals who, for a time, dominated such businesses—the Vanderbilts, Harrimans, Rockefellers, Carnegies, Fords, Morgans, and others—symbolized the giant firms that were changing the economy. Although other kinds of businesses, both then and later, exhibited some of the characteristics of big business, it was the "rise" of large-scale companies in those three areas (especially in railroads and manufacturing) that signaled the coming of a new economic order in the land. Indeed, railroads and manufacturing are the industries with which most of this book will deal.

"Big business" refers (at least here) to a particular kind of institution through which goods and services were financed, produced, and distributed. A big business was a very different economic creation from the businesses of colonial and early national days. It was structured and it functioned in new ways. These differences can be looked at from various viewpoints, but here they will be explained in terms of several basic institutional characteristics—those of the structure, function, and behavior of the businesses.

Most enterprises considered to be big businesses exhibited distinctive features. One obvious characteristic of large-scale enterprises was that they embodied much larger pools of capital than had the businesses of earlier days. In contrast, the typical business establishment of the first half of the nineteenth century was financed by a single person or by several people bound together in a partnership. As such, it represented the personal wealth of a very few persons. Most manufacturing enterprises (with the exception of some textile mills and iron furnaces) were quite small, involving little in the way of physical plants or expensive machinery. It was relatively easy to get into business, for the initial costs of going into trade or simple manufacturing were within the reach of many citizens. Business failures were frequent, but there was little social or even economic stigma attached to having failed unless the bankrupt person was thought dishonest; stupidity, but not deception, was repeatedly forgivable. Corporations were rare and business had a very personal tone. The fact that it was easy to enter business nurtured the belief that the society was open and fluid, that this was a land of opportunity. The goods most people bought were made and sold by small businesses, and because the capital requirements for most business were small, people could easily dream of owning and operating their own establishments. A great many people in antebellum America, it seemed, were in business, if only in a small way. "What most astonishes me in the United States," Alexis de Tocqueville recalled of his visit in the 1830s, "is not so much the marvelous grandeur of some undertakings, as the innumerable multitudes of small ones."

The investment represented by many of the late nineteenth-century corporations was vastly larger than even the grandest undertakings of the antebellum years. The buildings and machines of the later enterprises were numerous and expensive. The capital needed to build, maintain, and operate the many factories, warehouses, offices, distribution facilities, and other accouterments of big business was enormous. It was almost impossible to create and run such institutions without gathering money from many people. The investment represented by early giant enterprises such as Standard Oil, American Tobacco, Swift & Company, and the various large railroads such as the Pennsylvania and the Baltimore & Ohio amounted to many millions of dollars. For example, the carefully researched study of Standard Oil by two sympathetic revisionist historians (Ralph and Muriel Hidy's *Pioneering in Big Business, 1882–1911,* 1955) showed the company's net book value in 1910 to be in excess of 600 million dollars. And when U.S. Steel was created in 1901, the aspect of the news that most amazed and impressed contemporaries was the fact that the firm was capitalized at more than a billion dollars. By way of comparison, the capital requirements of even the largest of antebellum manufacturers—the textile companies—was seldom more than a million dollars, and those of the vast majority of firms engaged in factory production before 1860 were very much smaller. The coming of giant corporations soon altered the old assumption that almost anyone could go into business and have some chance of succeeding as well as the next person. Anyone who sat around planning the creation of, for instance, another U.S. Steel in 1901 with the savings and credit of a few friends would surely have been thought a lunatic.

Another important difference between small and large businesses was related to the scale of capital needs just discussed. This related distinction lay in the different nature of capital requirements and costs for large and small firms. A business needed two kinds of capital, fixed and working, and it encountered two kinds of costs, fixed (or constant) and operating (or variable). Put in a highly simplified way, fixed capital or assets were those represented by a company's land, buildings, and machinery; working capital was the money needed to run the business once it was in operation. Fixed (or constant) costs were those borne by the firm whether or not it was producing—costs such as interest charges on the fixed capital, taxes, and so on. Operating costs, on the other hand, were represented by salaries, wages, raw materials, and any costs directly associated with production, distribution, and transportation. The small manufacturers of the first half of the nineteenth century found that their yearly operating costs were very high, often exceeding the initial expense of the land and physical plant. That is, working capital was much more important than was fixed capital for most early businesses. Merchants and small artisan-entrepreneurs had even less in the way of fixed capital and fixed costs. When a depression or a recession struck, it was not hard for a firm to ride it out simply by closing down temporarily and sending the employees home. "When an article was produced by a small manufacturer, employing, probably at his own home, two or three journeymen and an apprentice or two," Andrew Carnegie wrote in an 1889 magazine article, "it was an easy matter for him to limit or even to stop production." Because the physical plant did not represent much capital, it did not disturb an owner greatly to see it lying idle. Even if the money tied up in the idle factory were invested in securities or loaned to others, the interest it would have earned would not have been a great amount. Because the operating costs were so high and the constant costs relatively low, antebellum firms had considerable control over when and under what circumstances they would continue to do business.

Because of the scale and scope of their operations, the situation for big businesses was quite different. A central part of the story of the coming of large-scale enterprise was advances in science and technology, which made possible mass production and mass distribution in many industries and brought about new processes in the production of metals, petroleum, chemicals, electrical products, automobiles, and other items. The new giant firms used complex technologies and many manufacturing plants, and they did so because the new production techniques made it possible to turn out huge quantities of goods at a much lower cost per unit. The coming of the complex new technologies and the multisite, multifunction companies had significant effects on the behavior of the firms involved. The many factories, mills, refineries, warehouses, blast furnaces, assembly lines, and distribution outlets represented enormous amounts of capital, so these firms experienced substantially higher constant costs than had their antebellum predecessors. This made it more costly to cease production when business turned bad. The extremely intricate interconnections between the various parts of a far-flung modern enterprise also made it more difficult to plan and coordinate downturns in production. Start-up costs were substantial, and market share might be lost to competitors during the slowdown. "As manufacturing is carried on today [1889]," the steel king Carnegie argued in the *North American Review,* "in enormous establishments with five or ten millions of dollars of capital invested, . . . it costs the manufacturer much less to run at a loss per ton or per yard than to check his production. Stoppage would be serious indeed. . . . Therefore the article is produced for months [or] for years . . . without profit or without interest on capital." Indeed, many of the new industries depended on high-volume, relatively steady levels of operation to achieve their low costs per unit of output. This made them inclined to keep the production lines rolling, which in turn contributed to the persistent decline in prices that marked the latter half of the nineteenth century and heightened business concerns about what many saw as excessive competition. Such factors proved to be significant influences on economic behavior and the rise of big business, as we will soon see.

These comments about the capital needs and complex costs of a big business point to another related and important difference between it and the smaller institutions of the more distant past. That distinction was the altered nature of ownership. The business enterprises of the early United States were usually owned by one or by several individuals, often bound together by ties of kinship and marriage. This familial aspect of antebellum business traced its lineage back to the earliest colonial days, as Bernard Bailyn's investigation of *The New England Merchants in the Seventeenth Century* (1955) indicated. Normally the owners of a business were also its managers. The owner-entrepreneurs made all the key decisions about the conduct of their firms. They knew intimately the needs and mode of operation of their businesses. They brought their sons, nephews, or talented in-laws into their firms to learn the details of the business, and when a firm's management changed, so often did its ownership. Almost all antebellum businesses fit this pattern, from the smallest storekeepers to the richest and most powerful families, such as the Browns in Rhode Island and the Hancocks, Lowells, and Appletons in Massachusetts. Because of the intensely personal nature of ownership and control, these early businesses often died with the passing of the owner or the lack of interest or absence of talent among the surviving members in the family.

Big business functioned with another method of ownership altogether. As economists Adolf A. Berle and Gardiner C. Means pointed out early in the 1930s in a book later enshrined as "a classic study" (*The Modern Corporation and Private Property,* 1933), a hallmark of the modern business enterprise was its separation of ownership and control. Because huge pools of capital were necessary, ownership usually had to be distributed among a great many people, and that in turn meant that the owner-entrepreneur commonly had no place in this new kind of enterprise. As the primary organizational form changed from partnership to corporation around the turn of the century, the number of owners (shareholders) grew so large that multiple owners had to turn over control of the business to one person or a few individuals. And as the complexity of management grew, the corporations eventually came to be run by professionals who had very little or no ownership at all in the firms they piloted. It became increasingly rare, especially after the beginning of the twentieth century, for the management of a major firm to remain in the hands of a single family. William Miller, in a study of the leaders of giant business enterprises in the period from 1901 to 1910 (published in a collection of essays, *Men in Business,* 1962), found that the majority were either managers who had risen through the company bureaucracy or outside professionals with special skills, such as lawyers. Once ownership was widely spread and management became the job of skilled professionals, the firm was freed from its old dependence on the money, talent, and health of any one person or small circle. It became virtually an immortal institution, easily surviving the deaths of owners and the onset of incompetence or disinterest in any single family. The rise of big business inevitably brought with it these fundamental changes in the nature and control of private property in America.

It also meant sweeping alterations in the spatial or geographical scale on which businesses operated. In simpler times before large-scale enterprises, many firms operated in a single town or city, or at least from a single office or factory.

Almost all manufacturing companies sold their goods in two ways. Some sales went to customers in the immediate area, and the rest of the product was sold through merchants in a nearby major city. For example, Baltimore iron merchant Enoch Pratt (through whose civic-minded generosity that city's public library system was later founded) sold the goods made by numerous manufacturers in Maryland, West Virginia, and Pennsylvania on the eve of the Civil War. The typical manufacturer had a very limited horizon, often living in ignorance of events and people in distant parts of the country. Retailers exhibited a similar insularity. There were, of course, some in the business world whose work did require a knowledge of affairs over a broader area; merchants who dealt in international trade had existed since the Middle Ages, and in the American context, bankers and merchants acted as the connecting and coordinating units in the economy. Such mercantile actors had to play on a wide geographic stage, extending credit, making collections, buying, and selling. The banking house of Alexander Brown and Sons, analyzed in Edwin J. Perkins's *Financing Anglo-American Trade: The House of Brown, 1800–1880* (1975), assisted commercial transactions all over the world from their branches in New York, Baltimore, Liverpool, London, and other cities in the decades before the election of Abraham Lincoln. Beginning in the colonial years and in the first few decades after the conclusion of the Revolutionary War, the general merchants of the seaboard cities, such as South Carolina's Henry Laurens, dealt with customers and suppliers all over the world. Despite that, their enterprises were not big businesses, but were instead very successful small ones, usually involving only a few people. Very few manufacturers, retailers, or others had substantial contacts outside the immediate area in which they did business.

This situation was overturned completely by the rise of big business. The giant enterprise of the turn of the century carried out its functions in a great many different, widely scattered locations. The old pattern of a single factory per firm gave way to one firm's having an array of production facilities.

As they expanded their activities, manufacturing firms and
railroads found their names becoming household words (often
preceded by barroom adjectives) in states all over the union.
The railroads laid their tracks and ran their trains over long
distances, with single roads or systems eventually covering
hundreds or thousands of miles and many states. Manufacturing corporations came to have numerous plants for the production of their goods, and later when individual firms di-
versified into various product lines, the number and kinds of
factories, mills, and refineries per firm were still further increased. As manufacturing corporations took over some of the
functions that had earlier belonged to independent businesses
(functions such as wholesaling, transporting, and sometimes
retailing), they operated in more and more widely scattered
locales. For example, by 1900 General Electric had numerous
plants in various locations and sales offices in twenty-three
cities across the country. By the early years of the twentieth
century, as Mira Wilkins has chronicled in several weighty
studies, many large American corporations had extended their
business activities around the world. Leading European firms
were forging multinational enterprises during the same years,
and "those of Britain, Germany, France, and some of the
smaller nations of western Europe began to invest in the
United States, first in marketing establishments, then in factories and mines," as Alfred Chandler noted in his introduction to Wilkins's *History of Foreign Investment in the United
States to 1914* (1989). Muckraking cartoons around the turn
of the century often depicted the leading business giants of the
day as spiders whose webs enveloped vast areas, ever ready
to trap the unwary or the helpless. As the cartoons indicated,
this new spatial dimension of business was disturbing to Americans accustomed to the older order of local, small, single-site
enterprises; big business, like the Deity the citizens addressed
on Sundays, seemed to be everywhere.

Not only did the coming of big business mean that private
economic enterprises carried out their functions on a much
enlarged geographic landscape, but it also meant that they en-

gaged in many more kinds of business operations than had earlier firms. Although the great colonial seaport merchants had handled a wide range of activities in the early economy, they were supplanted by a new kind of business after 1815, when mercantile operations became more highly specialized. A merchant tended to become primarily a wholesaler or retailer, an exporter or an importer, to have one particular kind of mercantile focus rather than a mixture of several. Furthermore, wholesalers often specialized in a single line of goods such as drugs, dry goods, hardware, or other articles. "By 1860," George Rogers Taylor wrote in *The Transportation Revolution, 1815–1860* (1951), "the organization of both foreign and domestic trade had reached a high degree of specialization."

Specialization had been even more characteristic of manufacturing operations. Manufacturers, whether small artisans or the owners of early factories, were specialized in function and in product; they were usually producers only and they ordinarily made only a single kind of item or a small number of similar goods. For example, an iron furnace of the 1850s normally made only pig (cast) iron; it did not convert the cast iron into semifinished wrought iron or into finished products such as nails or hardware. Separate businesses handled the processing of the cast iron—businesses such as forges, slitting mills, and rolling mills, none of which had any direct connection with the furnace. But in a big business such as Carnegie Steel in 1900, one firm made cast iron and steel plus a wide variety of other metal goods in its own rolling mills and forges. When mid-nineteenth-century manufacturers needed to market their products, they had turned to specialized wholesalers who handled the task of merchandising the goods to distant retailers or other customers. When producers needed to have goods transported, they had called on forwarding merchants or on the early traffic departments of railroads. For example, the ironmasters of 1850 would simply turn over the marketing of their cast iron to separate businesses (such as the one led by Baltimore iron merchant, Enoch Pratt), which sold the goods and charged the ironmasters for the services rendered. Carnegie Steel, on the other hand, had its own company sales force by 1900. Similarly, in the business of raising, butchering, transporting, and selling fresh meat, each step in 1850 had been handled by a different, separate business. By 1900, firms such as Swift and Armour were doing the slaughtering, transporting, warehousing, and retailing of beef, all as a part of the same company's operations. The economic system of the United States in the mid-nineteenth century was highly subdivided, and each business did its special task with little knowledge of related activities.

The modern manufacturing corporation altered that earlier system by expanding the range of a firm's functions and its products. Big businesses often combined under a single corporate roof the activities of obtaining raw materials, turning them into manufactured products, wholesaling the goods, and sometimes retailing them, as Glenn Porter and Harold C. Livesay demonstrated by examining a number of major corporations in *Merchants and Manufacturers* (1971). Many corporations also came to have their own internal traffic departments which handled the transportation of goods, sometimes via the companies' own fleets of trucks, ships, or railroad cars (Swift & Co. and Standard Oil are good examples). And many large businesses were also able to achieve a high degree of autonomy in the financial sphere as well, paying for improvements or new operations out of earlier earnings retained by the corporations, or issuing stocks or bonds whose acceptance rested more on the strength of the businesses than on the reputation of the bankers who underwrote the issues. In 1850 such financial independence was rare. An ironmaster or meatpacker had to rely for loans on separate businesses such as banks or big wholesalers. Antebellum merchants often loaned substantial amounts to manufacturers, and some merchants eventually transferred their skills into the field of banking, as illustrated by Elva Tooker's study of a Philadelphia metal merchant, *Nathan Trotter* (1955). By 1900, however, firms like Carnegie Steel and Armour & Co. were strong enough to enjoy

a significant degree of independence from such outside financial sources.

The coming of big business saw an accumulation of various different economic functions within a single company
(often called vertical integration), and unification made business units much more powerful and much more the masters
of their own economic fate. The leaders of giant firms found
themselves freer to act and more able to control the course of
their enterprises with "everything being within ourselves," as
Andrew Carnegie once phrased it. As they multiplied their
functions, so too did large-scale enterprises increase their range
of products. Many of the new businesses abandoned the traditional pattern of narrow specialization and turned to the
production of several different kinds of goods, especially as
the twentieth century progressed. Some of the largest, most
complex, and successful businesses in America and in Western
Europe had learned before World War I to apply their talents
and production facilities to a diversity of products within a
single firm.

The proliferation of factories, the geographical growth of
firms, the increasing variety of products, and most especially
the integration of different areas of business within one enterprise necessitated a complete change in the way businesses
were run. In the days before giant enterprises, businesses required very little in the way of administrative networks. Mercantile, commercial, and financial enterprises usually involved
only a few partners and a handful of clerks who had a knowledge of bookkeeping and could write in the flowing, clear,
formal business penmanship so useful in avoiding misunder-
standings in the age before the typewriter and the word pro-
cessor. The small manufacturing shops, peopled by an artisan-
entrepreneur and a few workers or apprentices, likewise required little in the way of administration. Even the factories
that arose before the Civil War involved only a manager, a
few foremen, and a group of workers who normally all labored
in the same building. Under such circumstances, it was relatively easy for owners or managers to oversee personally al-

most all the operations of their businesses. When something went wrong or could be improved, the bosses had only to shout out their wishes to the few workers who took orders at the mill or the office. Similarly, because businesses seldom operated in more than one location, there were almost no problems of controlling distant operations. The only figures in business who normally engaged in activities in widely separated areas were the large merchants and bankers, and they tried to insure accountability and honesty in distant branches by staffing them with relatives. Few concerns, however, had any such problems with the oversight of the firm or factory; those sorts of administrative challenges rarely arose before the advent of large-scale corporations.

As big businesses appeared in the economy, however, they brought with them new administrative problems and the need for new managerial patterns. How could owners or managers know what was going on in the various locales? How could they make their decisions known to distant employees and see that they were effectively carried out? As the number of different kinds of functions performed by a single firm increased, the difficulties grew even more complex. How could the needs and capacities of the various divisions of the firm be ascertained and coordinated? How could the purchasing department supply the right amount and kinds of raw materials in the right sequence to be sure the factories or mills could function efficiently? How could the marketing activities be geared to the rate of production so as to insure a rational flow of goods into the market and thus minimize fluctuations in prices and profits? The success of the venture depended on a great many separate but interrelated activities, all of which had to be managed well to see that the internal rhythm of the enterprise was intelligently controlled and coordinated. Everything was contingent on something else, and it was all scattered about the landscape. No one individual could possibly oversee the operation personally.

The solutions to the new and perplexing problems of management could be found only through the creation of elaborate, formal administrative networks, the bureaucracies that are the characteristic organizational form in the modern world. To work efficiently, business had to be carefully organized, with various levels of managers making and implementing both the long-range planning for the venture as a whole and the day-to-day operations of its far-flung divisions. Formal, written rules were created to govern affairs ranging from the selection of qualified personnel to the operation of the production and distribution processes to the procedures for firing top managers and clerks. Clear lines of authority and control had to be devised so that people understood their roles, responsibilities, authority, and accountability. Only by building such an elaborate administrative network was it possible for big business to avoid chaos.

A major challenge was devising systems and technologies for handling the enormous volume of information generated within a modern firm. Intelligent management requires accurate, comprehensible, retrievable data, in vast quantities. As JoAnne Yates's *Control through Communication: The Rise of System in American Management* (1989) demonstrated by examining the history of Du Pont, the Illinois Central Railroad, and the Scoville Manufacturing Company, it was not easy to work out the means through which information and communications could flow down, up, and laterally throughout a complex business. The storage, summary, and retrieval of massive amounts of data presented a thorny problem for a business system accustomed to keeping its meager records in a few handwritten volumes and boxes of correspondence. Generations of new typing and copying devices began to evolve, along with new filing and storage systems, to satisfy the organization's voracious requirements for information and communications. With big business began a communications revolution that would in time produce the computer.

When business innovators began to create large-scale enterprises in the last half of the nineteenth century, they were usually unaware of these administrative problems at first. Often the results were chaotic. Rather than reaping the benefits of expanded and dispersed operations, they sometimes found themselves encountering losses as a result of their inability to solve complex managerial problems. The transition to big business was often a troubled, painful, experimental process that produced more failures than successes. Many prominent railroads had gone bankrupt and been reorganized several times by the 1890s, and many of the early combinations in manufacturing were complete failures. Because the institution of big business was new, those who built large corporations had to feel their way through the early years. Because they were trying something novel, they had very few sources of informed and experienced assistance. Only after businesses had arisen whose size and complexity called for correspondingly large and dense bureaucratic managerial structures did universities create graduate management schools in the first decade of the twentieth century to train people to run big businesses. Management became a very different and considerably more difficult job after the rise of large-scale business concerns, and the likelihood of a single manager's running such a venture efficiently became very small indeed.

As large corporations began to build the elaborate bureaucracies necessary for their existence, another profound difference between the mid-nineteenth-century concern and the turn-of-the-century giant enterprise emerged—business began to lose its highly personal tone. Almost from the earliest days of economic endeavors among the European colonists, businesses were extensions of the personalities of those who ran them. The way in which businesses dealt with other businesses—with assurance and respect or with misgivings and extreme caution—depended on the personal character and wealth of individuals. In large part, this was due to the fact that very few concerns were widely owned or were organized in corporate form. A business was worth only as much as its owners and their partners, and business success rested heavily on how others perceived one's character. Because the entire early economy functioned on credit (few were able to pay cash, and payment after six, twelve, or eighteen months was common), the confidence of creditors in an individual often determined the ability of that person's business to expand during good times or to survive in bad times. The whole ethos of nineteenth-century individualism and what today seems small-town morality was closely related to these interwoven values and attitudes toward business. When Lewis Tappan founded his Mercantile Agency in the 1840s (the country's first nation-wide credit bureau and a forerunner of Dun and Bradstreet), the credit rating of a business was influenced almost as much by the character and personal habits of its owners as by the firm's profits. The good owner-entrepreneur was sober, honest, diligent, hardworking, and shrewd—an amalgam of the old puritan virtues harnessed in pursuit of profit. Such people did not hang around saloons or associate with unsavory characters—or at least they only did so with the same discretion and shrewdness they brought to their leatherbound journals and day books. Firms were merely the cloaks which individuals put on to do business; as an antebellum phrase put it, a firm's name was simply the current "style" of those running the enterprise. Perhaps the clearest indication of the personal tone of business was the fact that it was common for a firm to die along with its owner.

Relationships between owner-managers and their workers were also quite personal. Because the managers saw their few employees frequently and lived with them in the same town, the bosses could at least be expected to know their workers' names, the quality of their work, and perhaps even some things about their personal lives. Large organizations, however, required layers of management, complex personnel functions to handle "human relations," and, in unionized firms, elaborate work rules and formal grievance procedures. The nature of relationships between the labor force and the managers, as well as the highly individual identification of persons with their firms, underwent considerable change in big business by 1920.

A necessary concomitant of bureaucracy was impersonality; a complex administrative network created a social and economic gap between those on various levels of the hierarchy.

As the operations of a single business grew larger, more involved, and more widely separated, employees often had no knowledge of the distant, almost disembodied people who controlled and manipulated the business and thus affected their lives so strongly. As more and more technologically advanced production processes appeared, work became highly mechanized and routinized. Management came to exercise increasing control over shop floor conditions that previously had been labor's domain. Work itself, as well as one's relations with others in the organization, grew more impersonal.

This impersonality spread to the owners and managers as well. As ownership was diffused among many people via incorporation and public purchase of stock, businesses began to lose their aura of identification with a single owner or with several partners. Corporations became potentially immortal institutions whose owners were numerous, changing, and not easily identified. As professional managers with little ownership rose to positions of power in the corporate world, many firms assumed an air of anonymity and impersonality. The importance of character and individual reliability in business dealings diminished as a company assumed a life of its own apart from that of the persons who staffed and served it. As anyone who has ever dealt with a modern bureaucracy understands, one could no longer simply go in and settle a dispute or misunderstanding by exchanging some straight talk with the owner. The locus of power and responsibility often seemed as elusive as the Cheshire cat in Wonderland, despite (and, paradoxically, also because of) the elaborate rules, the standardized procedures, and the supposedly clear lines of authority and control.

The years of the rise of big business did not, alas, present an entirely unambiguous picture of the shift from a highly personal to a very impersonal business world. As is always the case, events do not conform easily to the generalizations historians offer to try to make sense of the past. Although the years 1860–1920 did mark the rise of the modern, impersonal corporation, they also seem in many ways to be the most highly personalized era in the entire history of American business. During the transitional period between the origin of firms that became modern giant enterprises and the subsequent triumph of diffused ownership and professional management, there emerged that fascinating generation so intimately associated in the public mind with the coming of big business. The era of the "trusts" was conceptualized by Americans of the time (and by many later historians) in terms of the business leaders who symbolized the early giant corporations—magnates like John D. Rockefeller, Gustavus Swift, Philip Armour, James B. Duke, Henry Havemeyer, Andrew Carnegie, William Vanderbilt, and the biggest and boldest of them all, John Pierpont Morgan.

It is not hard to understand why it seemed an age of business titans, robber barons, and industrial giants. First, there was considerable justification for thinking of the corporations in terms of the founders, at least for a time. They usually held a large chunk of ownership, if not a controlling interest, and many of them did at first play central managerial roles in their enterprises. Furthermore, it seems to be almost a universal human trait to adopt the mental shorthand of identifying if possible a single person with the larger entity, especially if that entity is thought to be evil; Hitler symbolized the whole of Nazi Germany, the Bank of the United States was "Biddle's Bank," and so on. The large railroads and the pioneering manufacturing corporations such as Standard Oil, American Sugar, American Tobacco, and others seemed even larger than life and more awesomely powerful than they actually were, simply because they were the first such institutions Americans had seen. They were novel and unfamiliar, and the people who symbolized them seemed all the more mysteriously grand and ominously impressive as a result.

Of course, in no case did any of the legendary business giants really control directly many of the numerous and varied activities of the enterprises associated with their names. It was impossible for those at the top to penetrate very far into complex bureaucracies; such operations depended on many people.

And those who provided the initial innovative idea or the leadership to launch a big business often found their degree of ownership and control diminishing as the firms grew. James B. Duke, for example, learned that he had to share control of American Tobacco with outside bankers and financiers well before the government's successful antitrust suit was completed in 1911. After a national market for industrial securities arose in the 1890s, and as management increasingly became the province of skilled professionals, even the public vision of big business leaders began to blur. (Growing anonymity may have been a factor in the decline in the public's criticism of big business after the mid-1890s that was documented in Louis Galambos, *The Public Image of Big Business in America, 1880–1940*, 1975.) In reality, the generation of giants (the lords of creation, Frederick Lewis Allen called some of them) acted as midwives in the birth of the modern corporation. Their achievements were great, their talents considerable, and their fortunes enormous. But if they had not called forth the new institution of large-scale business enterprise, others would have, for its time had clearly come. In this sense, their personal stamp on the era is illusory, for the businesses they began quickly outgrew their ability to control or manage them. The impersonal, institutional demands of giant firms shaped new patterns of ownership and management by the opening years of the twentieth century, eclipsing the brief but exceedingly bright glow of the generation whose names had for a time symbolized big business.

Whether the giant corporations were personal or impersonal, a final aspect of big business that should be noted is that they represented very great conglomerations of wealth and power. Although the business world before 1850 produced some extremely rich individuals and some influential companies, it had nothing comparable to the accumulated wealth and power embodied in the huge firms of the late nineteenth and early twentieth centuries. Decisions made by the managers of giant enterprises touched the lives of thousands and could affect the course of the wider economy. A whole new middle class of managers arose with the corporation, and their values and influence soon supplanted those of the earlier professional, mercantile, and agrarian elites throughout American society. And a relative few became rich on a scale never possible before. They naturally came to have the power that accompanies such wealth in the United States. Although it is very difficult to judge whether the influence of business as a whole in American life was increased (it had always been great), there is little doubt that the rise of big business meant the concentration of economic and social power in the hands of a very few. Fear of that power and its relative distance from the democratic process in the political sphere contributed mightily to the misgivings that Americans felt about the huge new economic institutions that arose in their society.

The most important, defining characteristic of those institutions lay in the fact that they represented a different kind of economic organism, structurally and functionally, than the ones that had occupied the landscape previously. Only by examining the contrasting nature of business institutions before and after the rise of big business is it possible to understand the magnitude of the changes in the business world during the years covered in this book. A large-scale corporate enterprise, as we have seen, differed substantially from earlier businesses in a number of respects: its capital requirements; its cost structure; the nature of its ownership; the geographic scale on which it operated; its performance of a variety of economic functions embodied in a range of goods and services; its managerial and administrative requirements; its anonymity and impersonality; and its great wealth, power, and influence in American society. These attributes were the hallmarks of the giant business concerns, characteristics that explain what big business was, how it worked, and how it represented a new institution in the United States and in the whole world.

The coming of the new economic institutions collectively known as big business had fundamental and far-reaching implications for American society. The effects on our political history were immediate; much of the bitter conflict associated with populism, progressivism, and the New Deal resulted from the rise and spread of big businesses and from disagreements over the proper role of such organizations in American life. The emergence of other great institutions, especially organized labor and big government, can also be seen essentially as political responses to the rise of big business. Indeed, as was pointed out early in this chapter, much of the work historians have done on the topic of large-scale business firms has revolved around their specifically political significance. In a larger sense, however, the rise of big business was only the most visible manifestation of a broad range of economic and social changes that resulted in the emergence of modern America.

In the era of the Civil War, there clearly was still a rural, agrarian-based civilization in this country. It was much closer to the republic of the eighteenth century than to today's society. By the early decades of the twentieth century, that civilization had just as clearly been transformed into a corporate, urban, industrial one. The advent of giant, bureaucratically administered, highly productive corporations brought for most Americans changes in the nature of work, in the communities in which they made their homes and secured their livelihoods, in the level of their consumption of material goods, and in the quality of their lives. The society remade itself to accommodate to the requirements of the modern corporation. A new technical, bureaucratic middle class arose whose values and culture came to dominate and define life in the United States, which Olivier Zunz analyzed in *Making America Corporate, 1870–1920* (1990). People left the country and moved to the city, despite all the changes that that made in their daily lives, to get what they saw as benefits from the new patterns of working and living. If, as Richard Hofstadter once suggested, the most important fact about this nation's history is that it grew up in the country and moved to the city, it is vital to recall why the move was made. Americans embraced the new industrial, corporate order primarily because they saw it as a more promising environment in terms of their material well being and the possibilities for economic and social progress for themselves and their families.

Furthermore, this was merely the first wave in what would in time become almost a world-wide phenomenon. The United States led the way in the creation of a corporate, market-driven civilization, but other nations followed, some very soon and others at a much later time. National patterns certainly differed in timing and in the various ways in which the modern corporation rose to prominence. (This can be seen in such studies as Mansel G. Blackford's *The Rise of Modern Business in Great Britain, the United States, and Japan,* 1988.) America's economic, social, and political system provided an especially fertile soil in which the new, technologically advanced, complex, bureaucratically administered business organization flourished. For almost a century the United States would lead the world into this new civilization that emerged in the decades following the Civil War.

Much good as well as much that was not good has flowed from the emergence of our corporate, technologically advanced, urban (and now suburban) nation. Whatever one's view of the ultimate worth or shortcomings of the particular kind of world we have built, it is clear that the modern corporation lies at the heart of it. Until we understand how and why we came to have that particular institution, we cannot fully understand our society nor intelligently judge the desirability and the possibility of change.

CHAPTER TWO

The Appearance and Spread of Big Business

The Advent of Industrialization

When General Pierre Gustave Toutant Beauregard ordered the shelling of Fort Sumter in Charleston's harbor in the spring of 1861, there was only one sector in the economy that included firms that could legitimately be called big businesses in the sense in which the term was used in the preceding chapter. That was the railroads, and at that point in our national history, they were still widely regarded as an almost unalloyed good. By the time of the Supreme Court's dissolution of Standard Oil, American Tobacco, and Du Pont a half-century later, much of the American economy was dominated by big businesses. They had come slowly at first, appearing here and there in manufacturing by the 1880s, adding to the concerns that produced the Sherman Antitrust Act in 1890. The pace then quickened, and they came in a torrent in the last years of the nineteenth and the first years of the twentieth century.

It is important here to keep in mind that, although industrialization had its greatest impact in the age of big business, it had begun before large-scale enterprises appeared in manufacturing and continued in many medium and small firms after the spread of the modern corporation. The United States and Europe had moved decisively into the era of the industrial revolution before the appearance of giant, bureaucratically administered firms. Beginning late in the eighteenth century, new technologies of production, novel machines, and the classic combination of steam, coal, and iron had given the world powerful ways of increasing the supply of goods. Britain led the way, with the young United States quickly joining in the exploration along what Thomas C. Cochran called economic and social *Frontiers of Change* (1979). And, since the War of 1812, the American textile industry operated what can surely be called modern factories. Francis Cabot Lowell founded the Boston Manufacturing Company in 1813, and that firm created in Waltham, Massachusetts, the nation's first textile mill combining weaving and spinning operations within a single factory. Caroline F. Ware's classic book *Early New England Cotton Manufacture* (1931) documented the spread of similar "Lowell Mills" throughout other parts of New England where water power was available. In the initial decades after the passage of the Constitution, early factories appeared in many other industries as well. Along the lovely Brandywine River in Delaware there arose a cluster of early factories, including the water-powered gunpowder mills of what was later to become one of the country's largest corporations, Du Pont. New York City and Philadelphia (including their environs) became great centers of manufacturing in the young republic. Throughout the Northeast, particularly along the "fall line" where the drop of rivers and streams approaching the Atlantic provided water power, industrialization had its beginnings in America.

By the 1840s the factory was being adopted by many industries. Although American producers were slow to adopt both steam technology and the advances in ironmaking underway in Britain by the 1830s, the decades of the 1840s and 1850s saw the spread of steam power and great progress in the metalworking industries. As steam became available as a source of power for manufacturing, businesses could operate factories in new places, sites that did not enjoy easy access to water power. This made it much easier for producers to operate near or in urban centers that offered a labor force or a potentially large market. Similarly, manufacturers could choose sites closer to raw material sources if they wished. In industries such as the manufacture of firearms, clocks, and nails, Americans led the world into new methods of mass production using specialized machines, a set of arrangements that later came to be known as "the American system" of manufactures. At the London Crystal Palace Exhibition in 1851, the world's manufacturers displayed the best of their goods and machines, and the American displays attracted great attention and admiration. As Brooke Hindle and Steven Lubar indicated in their *Engines of Change* (1987), the American triumph at that first of the great international world's fairs symbolized the industrial maturity of the United States on the global stage. By the close of the 1850s, then, the American nation was well launched into industrialization and rapid, sustained economic growth. A strong increase in the demand for goods arose within the developing regional hinterlands as the population spread westward, and manufacturing centers such as industrial Philadelphia grew rapidly, as shown in Diane Lindstrom's *Economic Development in the Philadelphia Region, 1810–1850* (1978). The economy now grew at a rate consistently higher than in previous eras of history. While scholars have argued for many years about the timing and sources of the transition to faster, sustained economic growth, all would agree that the United States was well on the road to industrialization and virtually continuous, long-term economic growth by 1860.

The national march toward mechanized production and the spread of factories did not for a long time bring the appearance of big business in manufacturing. Even the largest of the manufacturing operations of the 1850s (mostly textile mills

and iron "plantations") did not fit the pattern sketched in the
last chapter. Only a few manufacturing firms had capital requirements that exceeded even a million dollars, and the vast
majority were very much smaller. There were no manufacturing operations of such magnitude as to include factories or
offices scattered over several states or abroad. Business continued to be done in single-plant operations, ownership of individual units was still concentrated among small numbers of
people, ownership and management still customarily went
hand in hand, manufacturers specialized in a single product
or a single line of goods, and industry had not yet become the
province of complex, bureaucratically administered networks.
On the eve of the Civil War the economy remained dominated
by merchants. Almost all citizens shared a belief in the overriding desirability of material growth, and the political con-
troversies over the power of big businesses still lay in the future. Of all the economic institutions on the American scene
in 1860, only the railroads qualified as big businesses, and their
time of great political trouble still lay ahead.

Pioneers in Big Business: The Railroads

Railroads brought new methods of management, new forms
of corporate finance, different dimensions in labor relations,
new ways of competition, and a new relationship between business and government. They also created the first modern corporate bureaucracies and recruited and trained the first generation of a new managerial middle class. In his *The Railroads,
the Nation's First Big Business* (1965) and in many of his
subsequent writings, Alfred Chandler made a strong case for
the pathbreaking role of railroads in meeting and resolving
many of the problems later faced by other giant enterprises.

   In the financial sphere, for example, the railroads presented problems on a scale never faced before in the United
States. During their construction in the 1830s, railroads, the
new form of transportation, had relied on heavy financial aid
from state governments (as had many canals earlier in the

century). The depression of the late 1830s and early 1840s, however, severely affected the states' purses and credit ratings, and the great railroad expansion of the 1850s had to proceed with less government assistance. The growth of the railroads in that decade put unprecedented strains on the economy's ability to mobilize capital. In the ten years after 1850, the nation's railroad mileage more than tripled, going from 9,000 to over 30,000 miles. By the end of that decade, Henry Varnum Poor's *History of the Railroads and Canals of the United States of America* (1860) showed that numerous companies had capital accounts of more than ten million dollars. Several, including the east-west trunk lines such as the New York Central, the Baltimore & Ohio, and the New York and Erie, were valued at more than twenty million. Most of the money to finance the growth of the rail system came from private investors, though some support came from the federal government and from states, cities, and counties eager to encourage the expansion of their transportation networks. Never before in the country's history had such funds been required for economic ventures; even the most expensive canal, New York's Erie, had cost only about seven million. The result of this new demand for capital was that America's money and investment markets were centralized where they have remained since—on Wall Street. The stocks and bonds of railroads all over the country began to be listed and actively traded on the New York Stock Exchange as the capital of investors in this country and in Europe was mobilized in support of railways. At the same time, the modern investment banking house appeared to handle the marketing of the new securities. Perhaps the earliest firm to provide the services now associated with investment banking, Winslow, Lanier & Co., began in New York in 1849 and flourished on the negotiation of railroad securities, as explained in Vincent Carosso's *Investment Banking in America, A History* (1970). In the 1850s, Carosso noted, such companies "contributed substantially toward making New York City the principal center of American railroad finance." As we will see later, a similar revolution in the nation's capital markets in the 1890s permitted and encouraged the flood of large industrial combinations around the turn of the century. The railroads, however, were the first businesses to require such large amounts that the savings of people from all over this country and abroad had to be marshalled.

The complexity of the railroads' operations also brought new managerial as well as financial difficulties. "Railroad managers," wrote JoAnne Yates in *Control Through Communication* (1989), "were pioneers in managerial theory and practice. They anticipated the systematic management philosophy in arguing for the need to systematize procedures independent of the individuals involved and to use systematically gathered operational information as the basis for evaluation and decision making at higher levels." A large railroad's activities extended over hundreds of miles and involved enormous problems of planning, coordination, and control. The number of financial transactions handled by a road's conductors, station agents, and freight agents required a central controller's office, begun first by the B & O. The scheduling of the flow of equipment to match expected demand over the system also called for new managerial structures. The long- and short-term capital needs of the giant enterprises had to be carefully planned, and the railroads became the first businesses to achieve modern cost analysis or cost accounting to anticipate financial demands and to measure the firm's performance, including comparisons between divisions, managers, and workers. These and other problems, on both a day-to-day and a long-term basis, called forth bureaucratically structured administrative networks to manage the voluminous, complex activities of the railways.

No manufacturing firms faced such difficulties until later in the nineteenth century. When they did arise in other industries, many firms turned to the management experience of the railroads as a guide. The railways proved a fertile training ground for those who later ran big businesses in the manufacturing sector. Andrew Carnegie was probably the most famous "graduate" of the nation's premier railroad, the Pennsylvania, to go on to another large-scale enterprise, but rail managers moved into many other kinds of companies because they knew how to run complicated, diverse, widely dispersed enterprises. The same was also true of other nations as well. When big business spread through much of Britain's economy after World War I, persons skilled in the complex challenges of operating the railways there were much in demand in other sectors of the economy. And when graduate schools of business administration appeared in the United States shortly after the turn of the century, the managerial principles derived from the experience of the railroads played an important role in their courses.

In some ways, the railroads were also leaders in forging new patterns of labor relations. Their workers were the first to operate in an impersonal, bureaucratically controlled environment, and they were among the first to achieve collective bargaining and grievance channels through their national unions, the railroad brotherhoods. Initially these unions, like many other early American labor organizations, were social and mutual benefit societies. By the 1870s, though, they were evolving into modern unions. Like many of the craft unions that formed the American Federation of Labor in the 1880s, the railway brotherhoods derived their negotiating strength from the fact that their members had scarce and hard-to-replace skills. A strike by such a union was a real threat to employers because it was extremely difficult to break the strike by bringing in outside workers ("scabs" in union parlance). Furthermore, the railway workers were empowered by the fact that they controlled the use and maintenance of expensive equipment. The unhappy history of unions that tried to include a very broad range of the nation's working people, such as the National Labor Union and the Knights of Labor, indicated that it was very difficult, if not impossible, to create and sustain unions unless the members had specialized skills like the railroad workers and the members of the craft unions that joined together to form the American Federation of Labor.

The giant corporations that arose in manufacturing, however, proved to be much more successful in fighting off unionization than were the railways. Most of the new big businesses came in industries that relied on semiskilled rather than skilled workers, and there unions found it extremely difficult to make any headway in the hostile legal and political environment for unions in America. Not until the New Deal, when the Wagner Act (1935) gave legal status to democratically chosen collective bargaining units (unions) and brought the power of the federal government to bear on employers, were industrial big businesses participants in the kind of labor relations found on the railroads in the late nineteenth century.

The railroads were also the first businesses to encounter competitive problems flowing from the fact that they did not fit the classical conception of many small competitors being guided by the invisible hand of the market as portrayed by eighteenth-century economist Adam Smith. In part this was due to their status as "natural monopolies." Once society had made the great investment necessary to build and operate a railroad between two given points, it was much less useful to add a second or additional routes between those same two points. As the nation's railroad network proliferated, however, it became more and more common to have just such competing routes. Often the only meaningful competitive weapon such railroads had against each other was the price of the transport services they offered. This encouraged price wars as different roads fought for the opportunity to carry the limited passengers and freight. This problem was worsened by the perception among railroaders that they already had such great fixed costs sunk in their systems that it cost them almost nothing to carry an additional car or two on any given train. They were therefore encouraged to cut prices, offer rebates, and use free passes liberally in order to persuade passengers and shippers to use their line rather than a competitor's. Almost any revenue, they thought, was a net gain, since they were running the trains anyway and their variable costs were negligible. As the work of Gregory Thompson has shown, this belief that the railroads had hardly any variable costs was wrong, but it became an article of faith in the industry, persisting for many decades and powerfully influencing managerial behavior. Since railroad leaders believed strongly in the notion of fixed costs, the idea exacerbated the price wars that were already ongoing as a result of the railroads' status as natural monopolies. The result was that the railroad sector came to have a constantly changing crazy-quilt system of rates. The public was alienated by this chaos and grave economic problems were experienced by the managers of this vital sector.

Such a situation could be alleviated only by some kind of cooperation between roads or by the creation of a central body to set and enforce consistent, reasonably fair rates in an effort to satisfy both the railroaders and the public interest. The unhappy state of affairs, in other words, could be relieved only by cooperation among the competitors.

The railroads attempted for a long time to bring order in their own house by joining together to create an American variant of the European cartel (usually called pools or associations here) whose purpose was to fix rates or allocate traffic between cooperating roads. This represented an effort to retain a strong degree of independence among the "competing" businesses, yet safeguard profits for the cooperating firms through private regulation of rates and traffic. Many types of pools or associations were tried, sometimes including provisions for fines for those who violated the rates or sought traffic outside the approved channels of the association. Later there were other cooperative efforts called "communities of interest" in which the roads bought stock in each other and placed representatives on each other's boards of directors. All these ingenious efforts were aimed at the paradoxical end of ensuring "fair competition" by blunting or avoiding competition. All were indications that, from the point of view of the railroads, the market mechanism was not working very well in their industry.

Although they sometimes enjoyed brief periods of success, almost all such efforts to control competition in the railroad industry eventually failed. That outcome was in part the result of the natural economics of the transportation sector, but it also had much to do with the fact that those overseeing such cooperative undertakings as the pools could not enforce their agreements through the legal system. At first the arrangements were not actually illegal, but they did not have the force of contracts, which the courts did of course enforce. In Great Britain and on the Continent, the legal systems were much more sympathetic to cartels, though the mere fact that a cartel's agreement was legally enforceable was no guarantee that competition could be controlled or profits assured. In the United States all such arrangements were voluntary and thus could not be enforced at law, and competitive pressures usually made it impossible to prevent one of the cooperating companies from breaking its promises by cutting rates or hogging traffic in an effort to better its own position. Rate breaking often was done in secret, through rebates in which a railroad returned a part of its charges to shippers in order to get their business. In addition, of course, railroad pools and associations raised very serious political questions about the fairness and legality of businesses conspiring to set rates through collaboration among theoretically competing firms. The fact that some shippers received unequal treatment from the railroads and thus had to compete under the heavy burden of higher transportation rates made the question of fairness even more urgent.

The political response was not long in coming. The railroads became the first major industry after the Civil War to be the target of widespread political attacks. Mercantile and shipping interests combined with agrarian groups to provide the impetus for a series of state laws in the 1870s that came to be called the Granger laws after the farm organization that supported them. The purpose of that legislation was to set maximum rates and to outlaw the charging of higher rates for short hauls than for long ones. The latter provisions were a kind of state mercantilism designed to force the railroads to encourage more business in those states through lower short-haul rates. In fact, from the standpoint of costs, it *was* usually more expensive per ton-mile for railroads to load, unload, and rearrange freight cars frequently for a group of short hauls than to route shipments on long hauls between two major rail points. As railroad historian Albro Martin wrote in *Enterprise Denied: Origins of the Decline of American Railroads, 1897–1917* (1971), "no rate-making practice was more firmly rooted in the economic realities of railroad competition." But this apparent discrimination nevertheless drew much public criticism. After the Supreme Court's 1886 Wabash case ruling that only Congress could regulate interstate commerce, the state regulations aimed at remedying situations such as this were severely weakened. Pressure grew for national legislation to outlaw pooling and to prohibit rate discrimination.

Additional public concern over the railroads had its origins in the unsavory financial wheeling and dealing of such railroad promoters as Jay Gould and Jim Fisk. Manipulating the prices of securities through what later came to be known as insider trading, bribing legislators and judges to gain a competitive advantage, and bilking unwary speculators intent on easy money, such buccaneers weakened some railroads and virtually destroyed others. These escapades inspired an early, delightful contribution to the robber baron view of the coming of big business, *Chapters of Erie* (1886) by Charles Francis Adams, Jr. and his brother Henry. "Pirates . . . are not extinct;" they lamented in a heavily punctuated passage, "they have only transferred their operations to the land, and conducted them in more or less accordance with the law; until, at last, so great a proficiency have they attained, that the commerce of the world is more equally but far more heavily taxed in their behalf, than would ever have entered into their wildest hopes while, outside the law, they simply made all comers stand and deliver." Congress responded to the cries for action in 1887, passing the Interstate Commerce Act.

The federal government's regulatory role was weak for a time, but later legislation during the progressive era (including the Hepburn Act of 1906, the Mann-Elkins Act of 1910, and the Transportation Act of 1920) converted the railroads into a fully regulated industry whose rates were set by the Interstate Commerce Commission. The peculiar competitive problems of the railways, as observers like Albert Fink had known since the early 1870s, could be solved only by some form of cartel, and the eventual political solution turned out to be one big federally administered cartel.

Although it is easy to see the desirability of control by a regulatory body that would take into account not only the railroad interests but also the public interest, it is also clear that the regulatory job done by the Interstate Commerce Commission was not a particularly good one. Albro Martin, in his *Enterprise Denied* (1971), for example, denounced the regulation spawned by "archaic Progressives," finding it so inept and harshly punitive that he blamed it for much of the later decline of the nation's railroads. Others would argue that the ICC was—like most regulatory commissions—dominated by the industry that was supposed to be regulated and thus was unable to do an effective job. Subsequent scholarship by Gregory L. Thompson, on the other hand, blamed poor management by the railroad leaders themselves for part of the industry's plight in the twentieth century. However one may choose to apportion the blame, however, it is clear that the difficulties of resolving the competitive dilemma presented by the railways were great and that the nation did not solve them very well. Clearly there was too much politics and not enough intelligent regulation or effective private management. Most of that story, however, belongs to the period after World War I, when railroads were unable to compete with the automobile, the truck, and traffic on federally subsidized waterways. For our purposes it is important only to acknowledge that the railroads were the first big businesses to grapple with the difficulties of competing in a setting where the normal market forces did not work very well. As a result they pioneered new ways of competition among just a few firms. Big businesses in manufacturing industries, as we will see, encountered somewhat similar problems, but the difficulties were not so acute

as those of the railroads, and the solutions were somewhat
different.

Preconditions for Big Business

In looking at the appearance and spread of big business in the
manufacturing sector of the economy, it is important to keep
in mind that there were two fairly distinct periods within the
general time span covered in this book. The first was the period
up to about 1895, which was marked by the relatively slow,
sporadic appearance of big business. Second, there came the
great explosion of mergers from around 1895 to 1905. By about
1910 much of the industrial structure of the modern United
States had been changed, and a great many of the giant corporations familiar to later Americans were established as powerful economic institutions. We will focus initially on the period of slow growth prior to the great turn-of-the-century
proliferation of large-scale enterprises.

Various conditions had to be met before the modern giant
corporation could arise in American manufacturing, and one
of the most important was widespread access to the commod-
ity the railroads were created to supply—transportation. Nationally oriented firms were a product of a national market,
and that did not exist until the country had a comprehensive
transportation network. Turning first to the early turnpikes,
then to canals, and then to railroads, Americans tied more and
more of the country together with increasingly reliable and less
expensive means of moving people and products. Much of the
subsequent success of the national economy rested on the existence of a large domestic market, which made the fruits of
industrialization available. That huge internal market relied
on a well-developed transportation system. After the comple-
tion of New York's Erie Canal in 1825, other states followed
in the construction of waterways designed to encourage economic expansion. The role of state governments in the construction of canals was very important, and the economic advantages of better transport were great, as such studies as

Carter Goodrich (ed.), *Canals and American Economic Development* (1961) and Harry Scheiber, *Ohio Canal Era* (1969) have clearly shown. Other cities and regions selected the newer means of transportation, the railroad. Cooperation between the business community of Baltimore and the state of Maryland, for example, resulted in that city's pathbreaking role in choosing a rail route (the B & O) rather than a canal to the interior. In a process described in encyclopedic detail in the *History of Transportation in the United States before 1860* (prepared by Caroline E. MacGill and others under the direction of Balthasar Henry Meyer, 1917), the nation's avenues of transport grew ever more numerous and lengthy. By the end of the 1850s, more than 3,000 miles of canals and 30,000 miles of railroads had been completed. Canal construction was on the wane by about 1850, but the rail network grew substantially until the close of the 1880s, totalling about 165,000 miles of road in operation in 1890. By the time of the explosive merger movement at the end of the century, in fact, the nation probably had more lines than it really needed as a result of duplication of facilities and expansion into some areas that did not have enough traffic to support the railways.

The importance of this transportation system to the coming of big business was considerable. Only a national market could call forth truly large, nationally oriented manufacturing corporations. As long as the transportation system remained crude and incomplete, the costs of marketing goods in distant areas were too high to encourage entry into those regions. Even if a manufacturer were an efficient producer, the high cost of carrying goods over considerable distances would add so much to the final price that the manufacturer could not compete with local sellers whose products traveled much shorter distances. For example, Norman L. Crockett's study of *The Woolen Industry of the Midwest* (1970) demonstrated that larger, more efficient eastern mills had no hope of breaking into the midwestern markets until shipping costs declined. "Transportation charges on eastern manufactures shipped to the Middle West declined steadily during the 1870s and

1880s," Crockett noted, "and in the process woolen mills in the region lost a substantial portion of their previous protection from eastern shippers." Such occurrences were repeated time and time again throughout the nineteenth century. The construction of a good nationwide transport system was, therefore, a necessary economic precondition for the rise of big business, because only such a system could create a national market.

It was perhaps also necessary from a psychological point of view. Earlier in the century, before the existence of good transportation, a manufacturer was simply not likely to think of penetrating distant markets that could not be reached by water. Overland transport was prohibitively expensive, except for the lightest and most valuable goods, and it was not possible to build a nationwide manufacturing firm until that situation was altered. Only after the country "shrank" because of the transportation revolution did people find cause to dream of building far-flung manufacturing empires.

The second development that was crucial to the coming of big business was a revolution closely related to the vast changes in transportation—a communications revolution. As we saw earlier, the late-nineteenth- and early-twentieth-century giant enterprise engaged in a great many different kinds of highly interrelated functions over large geographic areas. This implied the ability to communicate rapidly and reliably, and early nineteenth-century businesses simply did not have that capability. Communication by mail was very slow and very uncertain. Businesses would, for example, often send several copies of the same letter or bill to improve the likelihood of getting the message delivered. Improvements in the postal system certainly helped, but the real breakthrough came with the telegraph.

In the two decades from 1846 through 1866, the telegraph industry grew from a primitive system with a few lines along the eastern seaboard to a comprehensive web of wires connecting the country. Cementing an early, mutually beneficial partnership, the telegraph and the railroad marched together across the continent. Telegraph lines were built along railroad rights-of-way, thus saving the telegraph companies high land-clearing costs. The railroads, because they were complex, large-scale enterprises, found the telegraph essential to the intricate operations of their large rail systems. Moving steadily toward a private monopoly in those two decades, the telegraph industry emerged in 1866 as virtually a single firm, Western Union. As the industry's leading historian, Robert L. Thompson, pointed out in *Wiring a Continent* (1947), Western Union's services proved of much use to the economy. "The businessman, the banker, the broker, and the capitalist were enabled to operate upon a constantly broadening basis," Thompson commented, "as it became feasible to reach out over hundreds or even thousands of miles and obtain intelligence within a matter of minutes. The increased scope of the operations which the telegraph made possible was a significant factor in the development of big business and the rise of finance capitalism." The appearance of the telephone later in the century increased the ease of communications, but it was the telegraph that was the truly revolutionary invention. No other communications technology had an impact remotely comparable on the world of business, with the possible exception of the computer in the twentieth century. The great advance came with the introduction of the speed of electronic communications through the medium of the telegraph, and that opened new worlds to the potential empire builder. It was the improvements in transportation and communication that permitted the creation of the first mass marketers, including the department stores in major cities, the great mail-order houses such as Montgomery Ward, Sears, and the Larkin Company, as well as the first chain stores. By and large those mass marketers sold goods from the older sectors of the economy, industries where some of the distribution could be handled more effectively by the mass marketing specialists rather than by the traditional web of wholesalers and retailers.

The third and final precondition for the spread of big business outside the realm of transportation and communications was the appearance of an array of technological advances in manufacturing technology. As JoAnne Yates wrote in *Control through Communication* (1989), "the spread of the telegraph and of railroads . . . encouraged firms to serve larger, regional and national markets, while improvements in manufacturing technology created potential economies of scale." Advances in the techniques for making iron and steel and other metals, and for shaping and working them, made available powerful new machines that increased output. In an interrelated set of industries, as David A. Hounshell showed in *From the American System to Mass Production, 1800–1932* (1984), highly specialized machines for manufacture, finishing, and assembly brought vastly increased productivity. At the same time, as Alfred Chandler emphasized in *The Visible Hand* (1977), some manufacturers utilized increased amounts of heat (primarily from coal) in their production processes. In other sectors new energy sources such as petroleum and electricity fueled new industries. Advances in refining and distilling techniques called forth astonishing improvements in output and soon led to the establishment of the best-known of the early mass producers, Standard Oil. As the numbers of factories increased, so did the problems in managing them. Soon a whole generation of engineers turned their energies to the task of better organizing factory production, a development known initially as systematic management and later as scientific management. "As the new mass production industries became capital-intensive and management-intensive," wrote Alfred Chandler, "the resulting increase in fixed costs and the desire to keep their machinery or workers and managerial staff fully employed created pressures on the owners and managers." Soon they were led along the first of the paths to big business in manufacturing.

Vertical Growth

In the years before the beginning of the great merger movement in 1895, big business came to the nation's manufacturing sector in two fairly distinct patterns. One was growth of a single firm via vertical integration, wherein the owners of a business would perceive a large potential market and find that to reach the market effectively, they had to engage in new functions. That is, the business could not simply produce goods but had to do other things as well, such as move into the marketing of the goods. A big business usually engaged in a number of different activities, such as purchasing or growing its raw materials, fabricating those materials into goods, transporting its own products, wholesaling them, or even taking care of retailing them to consumers. A firm that did a number of different things was said to be vertically integrated because it handled the necessary activities on various rungs of the ladder reaching from raw materials all the way up to final consumers. If a company started out just as a producer of goods and then moved into marketing, it was said to have integrated forward (that is, closer to the end—the consumer at the top of the ladder). And if it moved into owning its raw material sources, it integrated backward (that is, further away from the functions at the top of the ladder). Some firms grew to be big businesses by expanding vertically (usually into marketing) and achieving such success that they became large and powerful corporations. This pattern of becoming or creating a big business will be referred to here as "vertical growth."

The other general method by which big businesses arose was "horizontal growth." In that case, a number of producers who all did the same thing would join together to form a combination of their interests. That kind of firm was formed horizontally rather that vertically, because it was an amalgamation of firms that all engaged only in production or transportation or marketing; the newly born combination was usually not engaged in the full range of activities on the vertical rungs of the ladder. Instead it arose through combination of similar businesses, all sharing the same rung on the industry ladder. When people spoke of "the trusts" around the turn of the century, they usually were thinking of the companies that began by this method of horizontal growth. Horizontal growth will be examined in more detail later.

This general division of the rise of big business through vertical and horizontal growth oversimplifies matters. Some large enterprises of the period grew through a combination of the two methods, and one could cite exceptions to the overall descriptions of the two growth processes. Nevertheless, the general interpretation of the two paths to bigness, vertical and horizontal, explains more about the rise of big business than other approaches historians have tried. Alfred D. Chandler's pathbreaking article in the *Business History Review* (Spring 1959), "The Beginnings of 'Big Business' in American Industry," was the first study to emphasize the vertical route to large-scale organization. Previous historians had concentrated on the horizontal combinations, but the usefulness of Chandler's more inclusive framework has been widely accepted. There is still, however, substantial disagreement about the basic motivation behind the creation of big business in the first instance and about the extent to which giant firms have been efficient and socially productive enterprises.

The big businesses that arose primarily through vertical growth were a mixed lot, more difficult to analyze than the horizontal combinations. Perhaps the most effective way to explain the process of vertical expansion is to say that these businesses usually began as producers and, in the course of increasing the scale of their operations, found shortcomings in the existing mechanisms by which they obtained raw materials or sold their finished goods. Those shortcomings led them to integrate backward or forward into functions they had not performed initially. In the process of meeting a new demand more efficiently as a result of their integration, some businesses managed to evolve into very large firms that clearly qualified as big businesses. The companies usually grew without significant mergers, at least for some years, expanding to greater size primarily on the basis of vertical growth. Their success often led others to follow their lead, and it was important to be an early competitor if not the real innovator who assembled resources in a new way. Because the successful innovations of one company quickly drew imitators, such industries usually came to be dominated by several large firms. That kind of industry, characterized by a relatively few large companies, is called an oligopoly, an unlovely word created by economists. Many of the nation's industries were oligopolies by the early twentieth century, and such concentration of production among a relatively small number of firms in an industry involved companies built by horizontal as well as by vertical growth.

Those who pioneered in the building of large, vertically integrated companies had usually encountered problems either in marketing their goods or in acquiring their supplies. Marketing was the more important of the two problems, at least in terms of generating big businesses. The merchandising system in use before the coming of big business was one in which almost all manufactured goods except those sold to local customers were marketed through independent wholesale merchants. This same web of commercial agents tied the economy together, gathering goods from a number of producers and distributing them to a diffuse market of relatively small and scattered buyers. The independent merchants also extended credit to manufacturers, arranged for the transportation of goods, and performed other services, all of which made them the wealthiest and most powerful group of business figures in the country. They played vital roles in encouraging manufactures and in backing internal improvements in transportation and communications. The merchants' control over marketing rested on the nature of products and of markets, and independent wholesalers met the needs of manufacturers very well as long as the products in which they dealt required only storage and shipping, without special complications in transport or handling.

Once products appeared that called for special handling or particular marketing expertise, however, the merchants proved less useful. Perishable or technologically complex goods both presented real difficulties for a marketing network geared to items that stored fairly well for long periods and that necessitated no expertise or demonstrations. Goods that called for new marketing techniques appeared in a number of industries in the last half of the nineteenth century and the early years of the twentieth. Those changes in the nature of products sometimes led innovative producers to integrate forward because they could handle their own merchandising better than could the old mercantile system.

Similarly, alterations in manufacturers' needs for raw materials or semifinished products encouraged some firms to integrate backward toward those sources. In the antebellum economy, manufacturers had learned to live with the difficulties of procuring supplies through independent merchants. Once businesses began to produce on a larger scale, with a range of highly interdependent activities, they began to feel increasingly vulnerable because they had so little control over their supply sources. Mass production called for a steady stream of large quantities of raw materials, and the old fluctuations in supply (and consequently in cost) became less tolerable. In order to assure themselves of adequate supplies at reasonably stable costs to make for a smoother flow of materials through the production and distribution process, some manufacturers integrated backward. Makers of iron and steel, for example, bought lands with ore deposits or coal to guard against the ups and downs of the open market in iron ore or fuels. Another reason for backward integration was to achieve a more uniform quality of raw materials. The latter case was most frequent in industries that relied on technologically complex or science-based production, such as the refining of petroleum or the manufacturing of iron and steel. Backward integration, then, was seen both as a means of gaining more control over erratic markets for supplies and as a way to improve quality control. Integration became a key element in the growing effort to substitute what Alfred Chandler called the visible hand of management for the erratic, uncontrolled, invisible hand of the market. By examining in a bit more detail the experience of several big businesses that appeared through vertical growth, we will be able to understand this route to bigness better.

One of the most striking illustrations of the coming of big business via vertical growth can be seen in the history of the meatpacking industry. In the decades before the 1870s, beef was produced and consumed largely on a local basis only. Thus the meatpacking business initially consisted of numerous relatively small companies that slaughtered and packed pork in the great midwestern centers of the industry, especially Cincinnati and Chicago. Packers would cure the pork or ship it in brine over considerable distances. When the long-distance trade in beef began, however, it was handled differently. Beef was not cured or pickled, so the meat did not stay fresh for very long after slaughtering, and the result was that cattle were shipped on the hoof by rail from the midwestern stockyard centers such as Omaha, Kansas City, and Chicago. The railroads built vast, widespread facilities to handle the movement of cattle from the West to the urban centers in the East. Once the animals arrived in the East, they were slaughtered and sold by local butchers. A great opportunity awaited the entrepreneur who could devise and implement a more efficient way to handle this trade.

That person turned out to be Gustavus Swift. Swift perceived (as did a few others) that if the cattle could be slaughtered and prepared in the midwestern stockyard areas and then shipped to distant markets, considerable savings could be achieved. At the western end, large numbers of animals could be systematically and efficiently butchered in large-scale slaughterhouses, which would reduce the costs of preparing the beef for market. More savings would result when the beef was shipped because only ready-to-market meat (called dressed beef) was transported, not the entire animal with its inedible parts as well as the meat. The success of any such plan depended first on improvements in the technology of refrigeration, and Swift watched with interest the early experimental shipments of dressed beef in the 1870s. The imperfect refrigerated rail cars of those years, as shown in Oscar E. Anderson's

Refrigeration in America (1953), quickly gave way to much better, more reliable ones.

Swift, who had come to Chicago in 1875 as a buyer for a Boston meat concern, soon became convinced that with improved refrigeration he could successfully market dressed beef. In 1878 he formed a new business, attempting to implement his ideas. The concern faced a number of problems in displacing the old set of arrangements among shippers, eastern butchers, and the railroads, which had substantial investments in facilities to handle the movement of live cattle. By exploiting the competition between the railroads, as Mary Yeager's *Competition and Regulation: The Development of Oligopoly in the Meat Packing Industry* (1981) has demonstrated, Swift was able to get his products shipped by rail to eastern cities in his own refrigerated cars. The real problem, though, lay with the distribution network.

In order to make his plans work, Swift needed not only shipping facilities but refrigerated warehouses to store the beef once it arrived. He could not simply have it unloaded on the streets of New York on a summer's day and then wait for buyers. The existing wholesale marketing arrangements for fresh meat were of no use to him, because they did not include the refrigerated facilities he required. He was thus forced to build a network of branch houses to store and sell chilled beef. During the 1880s, Swift & Company created a nationwide web of the necessary facilities, often forming partnerships with local jobbers willing to join the new venture. Once Swift overcame initial consumer resistance to meat slaughtered days before in distant places, his products found a booming market because they were as good as freshly butchered meats and were substantially cheaper.

After Swift's integration into marketing, the company quickly became a complex big business. The firm's purchases of live animals, the activities of its large slaughtering and butchering plants in the Midwest, and the transport of its dressed beef all had to be coordinated very carefully to match the fluctuating demand in the cities where the meat was con-

sumed. Swift & Company was an early user of telegraph services to allow rapid communication between its far-flung operations. Before the merger wave of the 1890s, the firm had
created a vertically integrated big business as a result of the
expansion into marketing made necessary by the shortcomings
of the existing distribution network, exposed by the introduction of a new and better idea.

Swift's success quickly attracted imitators anxious to cash
in on the new trade. By the 1890s, competitors like Philip
Armour had followed on Swift's heels and had carved out a
share of the market by building similar, integrated businesses.
It was not, however, a game that very many could play successfully. The size of the market was large but not infinite, and
there was a premium on getting in early. This meant that the
industry would be dominated by a few, large firms rather than
by many small enterprises as in the older order. It was to
become a common pattern in many industries.

Critics soon began including the "Beef Trust" on their list
of concentrated industries. The meatpackers in fact had to
overcome collusion among opponents with vested interests in
the less efficient, old order. Nevertheless the giant meatpackers
became the target of one of the era's earliest "muckrakers,"
Upton Sinclair. In his novel *The Jungle* (1906), Sinclair portrayed the drudgery and hopelessness of the slaughterhouse
workers and sounded a plea for socialism, dedicating his book
to the workers of America. Most public criticism focused not
on working conditions in the industry, but on the collusion of
big packers. The results of a federal investigation published in
1905 (the *Report of the Commissioner of Corporations on the
Beef Industry*), though, indicated little evidence of illegal activity by Swift and other meatpackers. Swift's company, like
those of his quick competitors such as Armour, had not in fact
evolved into a big business by absorbing or colluding with
other meatpackers—instead, it had grown through internal expansion begun by integration into marketing.

Another firm that rose to national significance after integrating forward to market a perishable item was the United

Fruit Company. That firm experienced its growth during the height of the merger movement at the turn of the century, but it was not created by horizontal merger. Its history closely parallels that of Swift & Company and is a good illustration of vertical growth. United Fruit grew into a major business by making a new "product"—the banana—available to consumers in the United States. Before the Civil War, bananas were not sold in American markets, but by the end of the 1860s some shipments had begun to arrive in port cities. Because of its highly perishable nature, it could not be sold in interior regions. Even after steamships were introduced in the 1870s and 1880s to speed the hauling of fruit from the Caribbean, the poor marketing facilities inland largely restricted consumption of bananas to the coastal cities. The commercial produce network in the nation's interior lacked adequate warehouses refrigerated (for summers) and heated (for winters). The innovator who followed Swift's pattern to create a national market was a Bostonian named Andrew W. Preston.

Preston helped create the United Fruit Company in 1899, and as its first president he worked to build an integrated business that could overcome the shortcomings of the existing marketing system. The firm created a nationwide network of wholesale houses equipped with the necessary cooling and heating apparatus to allow sales in many areas. Within two years, distributing outlets were opened in twenty-one major cities, and business was booming. Within ten years of its creation, United Fruit had become one of the country's major corporations and boasted more than $40 million in assets. Although no Upton Sinclair appeared to write a novel depicting the less admirable aspects of its operations, United Fruit later became a symbol of United States economic imperialism, exercising great political and economic influence in what Americans sometimes condescendingly referred to as the banana republics of Latin America.

Marketing problems led others besides the purveyors of perishable goods into vertical integration. Early firms in the electrical industry, for example, created major businesses primarily through internal expansion and vertical integration. An intelligent strategy of integration was only one of the factors that explained the success of the industry's two giants, General Electric and Westinghouse. As Harold C. Passer's *The Electrical Manufacturers, 1875–1900* (1953) argued, both mergers and the advantages of monopoly over production opportunities resulting from the patent laws played important parts. However, the two firms that dominated the industry by the early twentieth century could never have grown large if they had not taken the initiative in marketing to overcome the inadequacy of the antebellum marketing system.

Though its origins lay in the preceding decade, the electrical industry emerged as a significant business in the 1880s. Thomas Edison's enterprises began in 1879 and expanded in subsequent years, producing both heavy industrial machinery to generate and transmit electrical energy and also lamps to convert the new energy source into light. The several Edison businesses were combined in 1889 to form the Edison General Electric Company, which in turn became one of the two firms that joined to spawn the General Electric Company in 1892. The other firm was the Thomson-Houston Electric Company, begun in 1882. General Electric's great American rival, Westinghouse, was founded in 1884 by George Westinghouse. All these early electrical manufacturers encountered very difficult problems in introducing a new product so technologically complex that the existing marketing system of independent wholesalers could not handle it well. The new industry found two major kinds of markets for its products. One was the growing number of central stations that generated and transmitted electricity to a group of local customers. This first market was the early form of what would later grow into the vast economic, technical, and social systems represented by giant electric utility complexes throughout the Western world, as analyzed in Thomas P. Hughes's *Networks of Power* (1983). The other early market was the "isolated system," in which a factory, store, or home had its own generator and internal lighting or electrically driven machinery, rather than drawing power from a central station. In either case the traditional merchandising channels simply did not work well in meeting the particular needs of the equipment manufacturers.

The merchandising difficulties sprang fundamentally from the new technological challenges associated with the product. First, the products were very costly and were dangerous in the hands of people who did not understand their use and maintenance. A number of disastrous fires, injuries, and deaths marred the early years of the industry because the destructive potential of electrical energy was considerable. It would not do simply to ship equipment to a customer and hope for the best, because resulting disasters would constitute what the president of Thomson-Houston called in 1887 "a serious drawback" to the wider introduction of electricity. The only satisfactory solution was to integrate forward into marketing by creating special departments to handle the installation of the goods, to instruct the customers thoroughly in the proper operation of the apparatus, and to take care of repairing the systems when necessary. Because the industry was so new, the manufacturers themselves had to take the initiative and supply a body of trained personnel to provide the necessary expertise and service.

The other technological difficulty lay in the particular needs of individual customers. Because the requirements of buyers were often unique or highly specialized (especially in cases where the electrical machinery was to be used to supply power for manufacturing), it was essential to have a well-trained force of company engineers to consult closely with potential customers. Westinghouse met this requirement by establishing, in the company's earliest days, a subsidiary engineering firm to market its products. Thomson-Houston (before it became part of GE) and Edison General Electric found it essential to supply similar services in the 1880s. By the end of that decade, the three major electrical companies had all established national marketing systems with sales offices and trained personnel who had the vital expertise to secure orders, install and operate equipment safely, and follow up with repair services and assistance. This was the same pattern that would be followed later by high-technology enterprises in the twentieth century, such as IBM.

As the history of the early electrical manufacturers shows, in new industries with extraordinary marketing needs, it was all but inevitable that producers would find themselves creating large, complex, vertically integrated enterprises. Their goods simply did not fit comfortably into a merchandising system composed of the old mercantile network of independent wholesalers. Expansion and the assumption of additional economic functions as a result of similar shortcomings in the old distribution network characterized firms in a number of other industries in the last half of the nineteenth century and the early years of the twentieth. Pioneering makers of such goods as harvesters, sewing machines, heavy industrial machinery of various kinds, and new office machines such as adding machines, typewriters, and cash registers often found it necessary to supply such services as demonstrations, consumer credit, and repairs. In many cases the manufacturers found the existing marketing network far too passive a means of pushing new goods into the marketplace; independent merchants were not accustomed to providing aggressive salesmanship and service on behalf of their many suppliers. In order to exert more control over the introduction of their new and complex goods in an often indifferent marketplace, the producers found it desirable to integrate forward and assume a more active and multifaceted role in distribution. When the automobile industry appeared after 1900, producers found that similar problems forced them to assert some control over dealers to assure the proper introduction, aggressive sales strategy, credit arrangements, and repair facilities for what was then a completely new, costly, and technologically complex product.

Some big businesses also grew in response to shortcomings in the system for supplying raw materials. Considerable vertical integration existed, for example, in the steel industry by the early 1890s. Andrew Carnegie's steel enterprises led the way toward integration during the 1870s and 1880s, as Joseph

Frazier Wall's *Andrew Carnegie* (1970) demonstrated. Carnegie marshaled capital and invested it in the latest, most technologically advanced production facilities. The dominance of his company rested on its ability to produce at lower costs than competitors. To achieve that position, Carnegie's enterprises operated on a huge scale and engaged in considerable backward integration. Steel was made from pig iron, and Carnegie resolved by the 1870s to control much of his own supply of that raw material. Fluctuations in the quantity, the price, and the quality of pig iron bought on the open market led the Carnegie businesses to produce their own supplies to feed their Bessemer converters, which in turn fed their rolling mills. Through the efforts of Henry Clay Frick, they soon moved even further backward, acquiring their own sources of iron ore, coal, and coke for fuel. Carnegie Steel even had its own fleet of steamships and a company railroad to transport its materials. James H. Bridge marveled in his *Inside History of the Carnegie Steel Company* (1903) that "from the moment these crude stuffs were dug out of the earth until they flowed in a stream of liquid steel in the ladles, there was never a price, profit, or royalty paid to an outsider." Because they found that they could assure themselves of a steady, reliable flow of raw materials and semifinished goods at low prices by integrating backward, producers like Carnegie sometimes expanded into new functions in order to make themselves, as Carnegie himself put it, more nearly "independent of the general market." In handling the enormously complicated tasks of coordinating, overseeing, and evaluating the activities of his many interrelated enterprises, Carnegie made good use of his knowledge of management and accounting practices first worked out on the railroads, as Harold C. Livesay argued in *Andrew Carnegie and the Rise of Big Business* (1975). Other steelmakers soon followed Carnegie's lead into integration and into the adoption of the modern managerial and accounting practices necessary to keep track of such varied and large-scale undertakings as a steel manufacturing enterprise.

As large, vertically integrated businesses developed in the American economy, they assumed a wide range of new functions and at the same time aroused fear and bitter complaints about their size and power. But collusion and conspiracy do not seem to explain much of their success, for most of these early vertically built enterprises grew without significant benefit of mergers or collusive behavior. In many instances, such as the cases of Swift and the electrical manufacturers, new and better products were supplied to a nation that embraced them as further evidence that theirs was an age of great progress. In a number of other instances, products such as those of the mighty steel industry were not only better than the ones they replaced, but they were offered at steadily lower prices, thereby benefiting consumers. One might condemn, as many did, the fact that workers did not share more of the resulting profits. One might also argue that the entrepreneurs received more than a satisfactory reward, as they reaped wealth on a scale not seen previously by private citizens. Nevertheless, the pioneering big businesses that arose through vertical growth appeared to owe their success primarily to just the sort of creativity, drive, and cost-consciousness that Americans professed to admire and to reward in their economic system. That is, however, considerably less true of many of the big businesses created through horizontal growth.

Horizontal Growth

The successful businesses that had their origins in horizontal mergers before 1895 usually went through a roughly common set of experiences. First, a number of manufacturers would enter an industry (often a new industry), producing goods in volume in factories that sometimes required quite substantial capital investment. For a time, all would be well. Profits would be good, and the businesses would expand, often leading others to enter the industry to share in the promise of prosperity. As the market began to fill up, however, producers found that they had to compete vigorously in order to keep or to enlarge their share of the market. Most manufacturers tried to do so by cutting the prices on their goods. After a period of sharp price competition (usually described as "ruinous" or at least "destructive" by the business leaders), they would find that profits and prices were not meeting their expectations and would begin to search for a solution to this problem.

Since most of those in the business world, like human beings in general, are prone to look for solutions that require the least possible change from their previous situations, they first looked for a way out that would allow them to remain separate, independent businesses. The basic problem they were trying to overcome was the difficulty of regulating production levels and prices in order to assure steady profits, as noted by many studies then and later, such as the essays in William Z. Ripley, ed., *Trusts, Pools and Corporations* (1905). If everyone would just behave properly, restricting output and maintaining prices, the days of comfortable profits might be restored. So, like the railroads before them, manufacturers turned to American versions of the cartel, a loose form of organizational control that seemed to hold out the promise of halting the overproduction and falling prices while at the same time allowing each producer to remain independent. Cartel behavior took many shapes, including so-called "gentlemen's agreements," pools, and the most common form, the trade association. Producers of, for example, steel rails could join together to form a Steel Rail Association to provide a convenient format in which they might agree to fix prices, set output quotas, or divide the market in some manner, such as by apportioning geographic territories among the members of the association.

From the point of view of the manufacturers involved, there were at least two things wrong with the association solution. One was that such arrangements drew political lightning like iron rods in a thunderstorm. After the Sherman Act became law in 1890 as a result of that political reaction, such cartel-like behavior was of very questionable legality. Perhaps a more important shortcoming was that the associations did not work very well. Although they tried various ways to enforce the decisions of the group, producers ultimately found that there was no consistently effective way to do so. A few producers almost always stayed out, undermining the efforts of those in the association. Furthermore, the agreements were always voluntary and could not be enforced in courts of law because they were not legally binding contracts. Under the common law tradition it was not illegal to make such agreements, but they were deemed hostile enough to the public interest that they were denied the protection afforded by the law to contracts. They could have worked only if the participants had strictly and voluntarily lived up to the terms set by the associations. But the temptation to cut prices and to try to conceal that fact by paying secret rebates to wholesalers or to other customers was eventually too strong for many. Downward fluctuations in business conditions often flushed out at least one greedy or weak manufacturer who wanted more than had been allotted in the pool. Another problem was that initially successful associations sometimes lured new producers into the industry, eager to join in the good times. Their productive capacity could prove the last straw, bringing prices and profits down again. The associations were, in the terse and contemptuous judgment of John D. Rockefeller, "ropes of sand."

Usually the next step after the failure of the association strategy was an attempt at horizontal combination, in which all or many of the major producers in an industry would form a single firm, at least in the legal sense. The first form in which this occurred was the trust, pioneered in 1882 by Rockefeller's Standard Oil. In that form of organization, a group of trustees (leading producers in the industry) received and held the common stock of different corporations in exchange for trust certificates, thereby effecting legal control by the trust over the properties of the participating firms. This legal device attempted to get around the common law prohibition against one corporation's holding stock in another without explicit statutory authority from a state legislature. After 1889 it was possible to form a horizontal combination by incorporating in

New Jersey, which enacted a general incorporation law permitting corporations chartered there to own stock in other such businesses without any need for special legislative action. This resulted in more and more combinations being put together as holding companies rather than trusts—a legal distinction that was ignored by the public and by many later historians. The popularity of the word "trust" resulted in its also being used to denote holding companies, as well as looser business alliances such as pools and associations. By achieving the legal status of trusts or holding companies, the new horizontal combinations were in a much stronger position to control the prices and output decisions of their constituent parts, and to begin to build new administrative networks to manage the giant enterprises.

Once the leading producers had formed a combine, however, the new corporation often functioned for a time as a loose amalgam of divisions that retained much of their former autonomy. This situation in fact amounted to continuation of the pattern of cartel-like behavior, because the firm's new central office often exercised little effective control and direction other than acting as a general forum in which price and output and market-apportioning decisions were reached. If all went well for the combination and the profits turned out as hoped, this loose kind of corporation might continue for a time. However, if trouble appeared in the form of competition from old "outside" producers who had refused to give up their independence by joining the combination, or from new competitors (sometimes foreign concerns), the combination was usually forced to take away the autonomy of its subdivisions and exercise more unified control from the central office. Often, the most effective way to maintain market position and profits was to become more competitive by ordering the closing of the less efficient plants, and by integrating forward or backward to perform marketing functions better or obtain raw materials more reliably or more cheaply. In that way, many of the firms that started as loose, horizontal combinations, however, evolved into vertically integrated, centrally administered businesses. Some remained loose combinations for a few years, and others collapsed and disappeared from the roll of American corporations. Most of the successful combinations, however, did become vertically integrated, modern big businesses. The general horizontal growth pattern just described was the road taken by a number of large-scale enterprises created before 1895 and also by the majority of the giant corporations built in the years after 1895, in the most explosive phase of the merger movement.

The behavior of prices was important in the process outlined above, and the general movement in price levels in the long stretch from the end of the Civil War to around 1895 should be kept in mind. Although the published material on prices is far from complete, a number of scholars have compiled useful data. The most widely used price series was done by G. F. Warren and F. A. Pearson, appearing in their short monograph *Wholesale Prices for 213 Years: 1720–1932* and in their book called *Prices* (1933), both based largely on data for New York City. Those studies and others demonstrated a broad, fairly steady decline in prices from the end of the Civil War to the mid-1890s. The wholesale price index for all commodities in 1866 (according to the Warren and Pearson studies) stood at 174; by 1870 it was down to 135, by 1880 to 100, and by 1890 to 82, or less than half of what it was at the close of the Civil War. Of course the pattern of declining prices was not continuous; in some years prices did increase. Difficult though it may be for us to imagine today, the overall pattern for thirty years was definitely one of falling prices. The wholesale costs of every major category of goods—farm products, food, leather, textiles, fuels, metals, building materials, drugs and chemicals, household goods, and distilled spirits—fell considerably during the years that brought the beginnings of big business. When manufacturers complained bitterly about plummeting prices and declining profits, it is clear that they were at least correct about prices.

To a considerable extent, the falling prices were a reflection of declining costs of production brought on by the spread of mass production techniques and important technological improvements. Before about 1870, as Lance E. Davis and Douglass C. North pointed out in their *Institutional Change and American Economic Growth* (1971), most industries were subject to what economists call "constant returns to scale," which simply means that while a bigger factory would allow the production of more goods, the costs per unit of output were about the same for large as for small producers. In many important industries after the Civil War, however, technological changes brought "economies of scale." This meant that a large, expensive plant could produce more cheaply on a per-unit basis than could a smaller one, as long as the large plant operated at high levels of output. The Bessemer process of steelmaking, for example, brought economies of scale to big producers in that industry. Other examples included petroleum refining and flour milling. Since such industries almost always saw the growth of very capital-intensive production, the firms involved experienced high fixed costs somewhat similar to those encountered earlier on the railroads. Economies of scale, coupled with improved management techniques and the existence of highly competitive conditions in many industries, brought reduced prices. Firms in such industries found that their high fixed costs and economies of scale meant that success lay in keeping the production process running "full and steady" to keep their costs per unit of output down. During bad times, they were willing to cut prices. As Andrew Carnegie declared during one economic downturn, "The policy today is what it has always been in poor seasons; 'scoop the market,' prices secondary; work to keep our mills running [is] the essential thing." One result of this sort of policy was, of course, more declines in prices.

The cumulative psychological impact of this long price decline on producers can be imagined. During the six decades before the Civil War, prices had not behaved in such a manner. Falling prices and periodic panics had occurred, of course, but never so relentlessly for such a long time. This steady downward trend in the prices received for manufactured goods disturbed and unnerved many in the business world. It was doubt-less an element in encouraging them to turn more and more toward cooperation rather than competition and helps explain the widespread tendency in so many branches of manufac-turing to search for ways of controlling output and prices.

In many industries, especially new ones or ones that en-joyed some kind of significant improvements in the technology of production, manufacturers initially found themselves in an enviable position. Growth was rapid and profits were good as the producers expanded to meet the demands for their product. Eventually, however, demand leveled off as the manufacturers grew to the point where they turned out as much as (and often more than) the market wanted. Then problems set in as firms struggled for a larger share of what had suddenly become an increasingly stable or much more slowly growing market. Prof-its might actually decline, or they might stop growing at the previously high rates. Manufacturers were likely to believe themselves in trouble and to start searching for a solution.

A brief look at one minor industry, the manufacture of wire nails, will help to illustrate the above pattern. Until the 1880s, almost all nails used in America were cut nails made from metal plates. By that decade, however, a number of new competitors making nails from wire had appeared and gained ground rapidly, with production levels rising steeply. By the middle of the 1890s, the wire nails had almost replaced cut nails in that market. The result was that the early growth and profits in wire nails began to level off, and producers began to find their situation less satisfactory than before. Recalling the years prior to 1895, one analyst of the industry wrote in 1897 that the "manufacturers had been fairly contented, making the comfortable profits of a new and rapidly growing business." When the pace of profit growth declined, however, the pro-ducers "cried out with one voice that they were ruined by competition." Setting aside the question of whether absolute profits really fell much or not, it is clear that the manufacturers found their new situation less pleasing than their old one. The first result of manufacturers' initiatives was not a genuine trust or combination, but a kind of cartel in the form of an association of independent wire nail makers seeking to set pooling arrangements to fix prices and output. For a short time after the cartel-like arrangement began, prices did rise. But soon prices declined once more, and the pool collapsed. The experience of makers of wire nails was typical of many other industries after the Civil War.

To some extent it may be argued that almost all industries that relied on factory or mass production went through something like the above pattern. In the textile industry, the nation's first factory-dominated branch of manufacturing, Louis Galambos's *Competition and Cooperation* (1966) showed that the earliest attempts at forming trade associations came in the 1850s, a time of declining profits. Because the factory or mass production techniques did not come to many other industries until after the mid-1840s or 1850s, one might anticipate that the period of good, growing profits in those industries would have lasted, say until the 1860s. The depression of the 1870s, coupled with the onset of falling prices after the Civil War, put strong pressure on manufacturers and probably accounted for the fact that the first widespread attempts by manufacturers to form pools and associations came in the decade of the 1870s. The search for reliable methods of controlling prices and output and therefore profits continued into the early years of the twentieth century, and it was especially common in new industries and in those that underwent significant technological changes involving high capital investment and high fixed costs.

It was just such industries, as Naomi R. Lamoreaux argued in *The Great Merger Movement in American Business, 1895-1904* (1985), that were the likeliest ones to form horizontal combinations under the stress of the depression of the 1890s. Lamoreaux emphasized that those industries were generally not characterized by "robber barons" or by highly creative entrepreneurs. Unlike many earlier manufacturers, they were committed primarily to "running full and steady," and there were generally fewer and larger competing firms in these industries than in many of the older ones. These mass production-oriented businesses constituted what Lamoreaux called a "new industrial structure," one particularly sensitive to the pressure of falling prices. Though not dominated by such compelling figures as the industrial giants that the public damned as robber barons, these lesser peers would follow organizational paths blazed by the pioneers.

During the three decades after 1865, then, manufacturers in industry after industry found their profits or growth rates unsatisfactory and turned to various forms of cartel-like behavior for an answer. Sometimes that behavior took the form of an informal pool for higher prices, lower production levels, or apportioned markets. Sometimes it manifested itself in a trade association, a somewhat more formal means of cooperation, yet one that still left each firm an independent entity, free in the end to pursue its own course if it chose to do so. Sometimes (after the formation of Standard Oil in 1882), it went so far as to result in a true legally unified trust or holding company that meant the surrender of autonomy by previously independent businesses. In contemporary public thought, all such attempts at cooperation were simply "trusts," the catchall term for any apparent concentration of economic power. As we realize today, however, only organizational changes involving the surrender of legal autonomy led to the kinds of firms that defined big business in the early years of the twentieth century.

Among the industries that between 1865 and 1895 definitely engaged in some form of cartel-like behavior were the following: textiles, iron and steel, nonferrous metals, hardware, petroleum, sugar refineries, tobacco manufacturers, lumber, anthracite coal, salt, leather products, cottonseed oil, liquor, glass, paper, gunpowder, and many more. The attempts at cooperation often began on a state or regional level and then later expanded to a national scale. Once businesses in a number of industries began to experiment with cartel behavior, others began to consider it and to try it out as a means of improving their economic position. This phenomenon of imitation also appeared in the great combination movement after

1895, as we will soon see. In the 1880s and early 1890s, however, relatively few industries produced real trusts or holding companies that turned out to be lasting, successful firms that became vertically integrated, complex big businesses. We will briefly examine three of the industries in which cartel-like behavior did result in a trust or a holding company before 1895 to see in more detail how the process worked. The three combinations we will look at—in oil, sugar, and tobacco—played extremely important roles in creating and publicizing the immensely profitable road manufacturers might travel if they could form a genuinely unified, legally binding "trust." The success of these companies (and a few others) paved the way for the flood of mergers after that date by fostering a widespread thirst to build combinations, a thirst satisfied in the turn-of-the-century merger movement.

The pioneer enterprise in the story of industrial combinations was Standard Oil. The importance of the rise of that firm was succinctly summarized by Ida Tarbell in her *History of the Standard Oil Company* (1904): "It was the first in the field, and it has furnished the methods, the charter, and the traditions of its followers." Standard was the first great horizontal combination in manufacturing, and no other company has been the subject of so many historical inquiries for so many decades. Henry Demarest Lloyd's passionate *Wealth Against Commonwealth* (1894) set the tone for most of the subsequent highly critical interpretations. Of the later studies, the two most thoroughly researched (and more sympathetic) works were Ralph and Muriel Hidy, *Pioneering in Big Business, 1882–1911* (1955) and Harold F. Williamson, Arnold R. Daum, and others, *The American Petroleum Industry: The Age of Illumination, 1859–1899* (1959). The evolution of Standard Oil, as all its historians have demonstrated, was a protracted struggle by John D. Rockefeller and his associates to bring order and stability to an unruly industry by imposing centralized control and reaping enormous profits as a result.

In the early years of the industry, after Edwin Drake drilled the nation's first oil well in Titusville, Pennsylvania

(1859), hordes of small competitors rushed into the new business. It was not a costly business to enter at that point, and soon numerous firms were competing intensely. Prices and the supply of crude oil and its refined forms fluctuated wildly. Three refining centers quickly arose—Pittsburgh, Philadelphia, and Cleveland, and from among the Ohio refiners came the man who eventually managed to organize the industry, John Davison Rockefeller.

The future oil magnate started out in 1859 in the produce business and entered petroleum refining in 1863. From the very first, Rockefeller showed a keen ability to choose able associates, and he became the nucleus of a talented group of financial and managerial partners. The Standard Oil Company was founded in 1867. By 1870 the firm had two large, efficient refineries that together represented about a tenth of the nation's refining capacity. Because his company was Cleveland's largest, Rockefeller was able to secure preferential rates from railroads anxious to haul his large, steady shipments. Thus began what would prove to be a pattern in which Rockefeller was able to whipsaw the railroads, exploiting their competitive weaknesses to his own advantage. He persuaded other Cleveland refiners to join with him to secure lower rates and better profits. Arguing that the other Cleveland firms could not compete with Standard's efficient refineries and its lower transportation rates, Rockefeller pressured them to sell out to him or face ruin. Early in the decade of the 1870s Standard Oil succeeded in dominating the petroleum business in the Cleveland region and turned its attention to national developments.

Refiners all over the country were growing unhappy with the continuing unsettled state of their industry. Manufacturers were turning out kerosene, lubricating oils, and other products in such volume that prevailing profits and prices seemed threatened by overcapacity. In order to improve their own economic position, refiners needed to achieve some degree of control over the production of crude oil, its refining, transportation, and distribution. Their initial answer was an attempt at a trade association, the National Refiners' Association, begun in 1872 with Rockefeller as president. This American version of a cartel included representatives from the major refining areas (by now, Cleveland, Pittsburgh, New York, Philadelphia, and the crude oil regions in western Pennsylvania). Those representatives allocated quotas for the production of crude and the sale of refined oil. Some of the firms pumping crude oil quickly formed a similar group to organize their end of the business. It soon became apparent, however, that their efforts were not working. Firms outside the associations refused to cooperate, and the agreements were even broken by the associations' own members anxious to get more than their allotted share of the business. The organizations collapsed, doomed by their weak controls and lack of enforcement powers.

Having tried loose alliances and found them wanting, Rockefeller and his colleagues set out to build a single big company to control the industry. Using the old Cleveland strategy of combining superior productive efficiency with rebates in transportation, Standard strengthened its position. Gradually, major refiners around the country were pressured or persuaded to sell out to Standard. Because they received generous rewards for their businesses in the form of stock in Standard, and because they could have a voice in the committee-style management of the combination, refiners sold out in the belief that profits could be assured by that company. These mergers were often kept secret, and the various companies continued to operate under their old names. By the end of the 1870s, a great horizontal combination had been built; the Standard Oil interests controlled about nine-tenths of the country's petroleum refining capacity.

The giant horizontal amalgam, however, was an administrative and legal mess. Because the law generally forbade one corporation from owning stock in another and discouraged a firm chartered in one state from owning property in another state, Standard was put together with a patchwork of subterfuges. Rockefeller and his compatriots personally held the stock of the companies controlled by Standard as trustees for their stockholders in an attempt to get around the law. By 1879 an informal version of the trust had been invented by Standard; a handful of trustees held the stock of out-of-state companies "in trust" for Standard's stockholders. Early in 1882 the arrangement was formalized by a Trust Agreement, and trust certificates were exchanged for the stock of Standard Oil. This apparently legal detour around existing laws was imitated in the 1880s by various combinations, including the trusts in sugar and in distilling. Growing political pressure and the appearance of New Jersey's 1889 general incorporation law giving blanket permission for New Jersey corporations to hold stock in out-of-state corporations made the trust form short-lived. It was replaced by the holding company (after 1889) as the favored instrument for combination.

In the years after 1882, Standard Oil faced challenges from both foreign and domestic competition, challenges that led it to move to consolidate its central control over the companies it owned. In 1884 the trust opened headquarters on Broadway, from which it directed the increasing integration and expansion of its oil empire. Most of Standard's market lay overseas, and the development of Russian oil by the powerful Nobel interests led to Standard's closing inefficient refineries and re-locating refining operations in areas closer to water transportation to cut costs and rebuff the threat from Europe. The discovery of new oil fields in the United States and the continual appearance of independent refiners led Rockefeller's company to integrate backward into the production of crude oil and forward into transportation and marketing. The creation of networks of pipelines to move both crude and refined oil was especially critical to Standard's maintenance of it leading position. Utilizing its efficiency, its financial strength, new technologies, and the harsh competitive techniques associated with its name—the use of rebates, intimidation, an espionage network reporting on uncooperative businesses, and ruthless vengeance for troublemakers—Standard built by the early 1890s a vast, vertically integrated company involved in every aspect of the petroleum business. Standard's near-monopoly position did nevertheless decline thereafter with the rise of competitors such as Gulf and Texaco in the new oil fields of the Southwest around the turn of the century. The Supreme Court's 1911 dissolution of Standard into a number of firms later completed the industry's transition into a business dominated by a few firms rather than by a single company.

Manufacturers in other industries learned with interest of the innovations of Standard Oil, and soon additional producers were trying to imitate its success in achieving control, stability, and handsome profits. Participants in the sugar refining industry were definitely interested, for their business was remarkably similar to oil refining. In the years shortly before the Civil War, major technological improvements in sugar refining, in the words of Alfred Eichner (*The Emergence of Oligopoly: Sugar Refining as a Case Study,* 1969), "had, in effect, created an entirely new industry." Those advances made it possible to mass produce sugar of uniform quality in large refineries for the first time. A number of new firms arose, built refineries with the latest technology in east coast cities, and successfully competed with the older Louisiana sugar companies. The period of the Civil War and the years immediately following it constituted good times for the manufacturers supplying the demand of urban areas in the eastern United States. During that initial period of growth, producers made "high profits" that attracted new firms and encouraged existing manufacturers to expand, according to Eichner's study.

By the 1870s, however, the industry ran into the troubles that afflicted some others in the same period—instability, falling prices, and declining profit rates due to the potential of the supply being greater than the demand. As the initial period of growth and high profits gave way to the price wars of the 1870s and early 1880s, the refiners' profit margin grew thinner and thinner. Because the industry was one that required large fixed investments, most firms were "no longer able to cover their full costs, if an adequate return on invested capital is included as part of their costs," Eichner reported. Investment in a sugar refinery was "sunk" into the plant and was difficult to liquidate or to transfer to other uses, so even marginal producers stayed in the business, adding to the problem of overproduction. Sugar refiners, like other manufacturers, soon turned to associations or pools in an attempt to regulate output and prices and thus restore high profits. The first counterpart to oil's National Refiners' Association was inaugurated in sugar in 1880. Despite elaborate pooling arrangements, these efforts soon collapsed, and for the usual reasons. Other attempts at cooperation followed, but they also failed. As a result, producers began to look toward combination.

After difficult negotiations, most of the big refiners reached agreement to form a horizontal combination, using the legal device Standard Oil had pioneered—the trust. In 1887 eighteen refiners joined together secretly and promulgated a trust agreement, exchanging the stock of their individual enterprises for the trust certificates. As in the case of the oil mergers, producers were offered stock worth more than they had thought their businesses were worth, and they agreed to join. Soon the sugar trust found itself exercising more and more central direction over the (initially) highly autonomous subdivisions, ordering the closing of older, less efficient plants to cut costs and raise profits. In 1891 the company took advantage of the New Jersey incorporation law and reorganized itself as American Sugar Refining, a corporation rather than a trust.

In subsequent years, however, the sugar combine found it ever more difficult to maintain its early near-monopoly position. A new raw material source—sugar beets—arose to compete with sugar cane, and the company expended enormous funds to counter that threat in the 1890s. In addition, it proved impossible to keep at least a few competitors out, despite American Sugar Refining's unsavory methods of competition. These practices included railroad rebates (by then definitely illegal) and attempts to strong-arm wholesalers into refusing to handle the products of any other sugar company. Such ruthless competition, coupled with the firm's traditional secrecy and the refusal of company officials to cooperate with governmental inquiries, gave the combination a bad reputation. Eventually this led to an (unsuccessful) antitrust suit. Nevertheless, sugar refining had by the early 1900s evolved into an industry dominated by a few large firms and not by one. As other businesses later discovered, it often proved quite possible to influence the course of prices when the industry was composed of a relatively few big producers. The creation of the sugar combination and the subsequent success of sugar refiners in restoring higher profits added further luster to the appeal of horizontal combinations in the eyes of other manufacturers.

The rise of the third of the major corporations we are looking at in some detail—American Tobacco—revealed a pattern strikingly similar to that of oil and sugar refining. American Tobacco appeared in the cigarette industry, a relatively new business (like petroleum and refined sugar). The industry arose after the Civil War and experienced a very high growth rate throughout the 1870s and the first half of the 1880s. During that period, profits were good and producers were happy. By about the mid-1880s, however, demand was leveling off, and the industry entered a period of stringent competition brought on by overcapacity. With the invention of the Bonsack cigarette-rolling machine and its introduction by James B. Duke in the mid-1880s, the existing production system of hand rolling became obsolete. Mechanization of the production process immediately expanded the potential supply to great heights.

Once demand leveled off and overcapacity set in, the producers fell to intensive competition. Heavy advertising was used as a competitive weapon, and by the end of the eighties, advertising costs devoured approximately twenty per cent of the companies' incomes. The manufacturers soon tired of this strenuous competition and began to search for a way to stabilize profits.

A few weak efforts at controlling output and prices followed, but with little result. During the discussions among the major producers about how to resolve the problem of overcapacity and costly competition, the alternative of a cartel with pooling arrangements was considered but rejected. The cigarette makers did not really attempt a formal association or pool because they were convinced that it was too weak a form of cooperation to get the job done. The earlier experiments with such arrangements in the railroads, and in the oil, sugar, and other industries, had clearly given such methods of seeking control a bad reputation in the business community. Accordingly, the cigarette producers decided after months of negotiations to create a horizontal combination.

The American Tobacco Company was founded in 1890, the first major combination formed as a holding company under New Jersey's freshly passed general incorporation statute. As did so many other combinations, American Tobacco at first operated with highly autonomous subdivisions, but its managers soon were centralizing control from the Manhattan headquarters and moving toward vertical integration. During the next ten or twelve years, the cigarette combination extended its influence into other branches of the tobacco manufacturing industry. Utilizing strong-arm competitive methods such as selective price wars (with what were called "fighting brands"), coercive agreements with jobbers to force them to handle only American Tobacco's goods, as well as the weapon of massive advertising to swamp competitors, the tobacco combine achieved control over the manufacture of smoking tobacco, chewing tobacco, and snuff in addition to its control of cigarettes. If ever there was what most people would think of as a "bad trust," it was American Tobacco. The federal government prosecuted the firm under the Sherman Act in 1907, and the Supreme Court in 1911 upheld its conviction, ordering that it be broken up into several companies. Even the smaller firms created by the dissolution of the industry giant were each of substantial size, however, and oligopoly proved to be almost as profitable and stable as the near-monopoly that American Tobacco had attempted to create. The efforts by manufacturers to control prices and avoid competition had ultimately led to a highly concentrated industry dominated by a few large firms—the pattern common among numerous industries after the rise of big business.

The motivation of the individuals who formed these horizontal combinations was clearly somewhat different from that of those whose giant businesses were created through vertical growth. Here the primary goal was to gain control over an industry in order to influence output, prices, and profits. Other purposes were involved, of course, such as securing economies of scale and reducing costs, but the overriding objective was improved control over output and prices. If that goal could be reached and maintained over the long run, monopoly profits could be won, which would be a burden to society. These early horizontal combinations provoked a troubling question, one that was to grow more pressing as businesses in other industries attempted to follow the lead of Standard Oil, American Sugar Refining, and American Tobacco: could market forces or political intervention assure that the social benefits of such combinations would equal or outweigh the costs? The economy was on the brink of a tidal wave of combinations that would make that question more urgent than ever.

The Great Merger Wave

By the mid-1890s the appearance and notoriety of various horizontal combinations in the form of trusts or holding companies had helped prepare the way for the rapid spread of such businesses. Once a few successful and widely publicized combinations had gotten underway, leading business figures in many industries began to consider the possibility and the desirability of duplicating in their own industries the pattern of Standard Oil, American Sugar Refining, and American Tobacco. In any sort of sudden, massive alteration in the organization of many businesses, the force of example is strong, and the new forms are "in the air" and faddish. The proliferation of conglomerates in the 1960s and of leveraged buyouts (LBOs) in the 1980s, for example, can be explained in part by the fact that they became fashionable. Before a major consolidation movement could occur in the late 1890s and the early years of the twentieth century, it was essential for businesses to have some successful examples before them. By the mid-1890s combination was definitely "in the air." Even producers who were not necessarily unhappy with their situations found themselves thinking of mergers, as did some manufacturers in industries where it proved impossible to gain and maintain control by creating large, horizontal combinations.

In addition to the growing force of example, a number of other factors must be considered in explaining why the nation's industries began merging in huge numbers just around the turn of the century. Changes in the legal environment seem to have played a contributing role in readying the economy for the rapid spread of horizontal mergers. One important development was the appearance of state general incorporation laws (such as New Jersey's in 1889) that allowed one corporation to hold stock in others without receiving special permission from the often politically hostile state legislatures. That change made it much easier to create holding companies and to fold together the stock of different enterprises. The new general incorporation laws, designed to attract industry to (or at least encourage incorporation and its associated fees as revenues for) such states as New Jersey and Delaware, meant that a company could obtain a charter simply by filling out a form and paying a fee. The new company could then operate in and acquire subsidiaries in other states without difficulty. These legal changes facilitated the rapid spread of mergers, as Donald Dewey argued in his *Monopoly in Economics and Law* (1959).

Probably of more importance was the role of the Sherman Antitrust Act of 1890 and its interpretation by the courts. One of the interesting things about human activities is the extent to which carefully laid plans produce unintended consequences, and the political opposition to the spread of big business was such an instance. Congress had responded to public pressure to "do something" about the problem of concentration in the economy by passing the Sherman Act. The Act was very vague, simply outlawing "every ... combination ... in restraint of trade." The intent of the law and of most of its supporters was to halt the spread of big businesses and collusive practices and to encourage a return to a more competitive economy of smaller firms. The particular way in which the law was interpreted by the courts, however, actually appears to have speeded up the appearance of the modern, integrated corporation in the United States. This was so because the courts ruled that forms of cartel-like behavior were illegal under the act, but that unified combinations were in most instances acceptable. That is, the law forbade collusion by independent firms but did not necessarily outlaw the activities of integrated holding companies created by the legal union of previously separate businesses. The result was that independent businesses were led from cartel-like arrangements to combinations in part by the legal changes originally designed to prevent the rise of more big businesses.

As William Letwin's *Law and Economic Policy: The Evolution of the Sherman Antitrust Act* (1967) showed, the legal thickets surrounding the place of cartel behavior and horizontal combinations in American law both before and after the Sherman Act were dark and dense indeed. However, it is clear that American law treated such issues very differently than did the legal systems of other industrial nations. The American legal system inherited from English law a strong distaste for cartels. Although cartel behavior was increasingly tolerated in England by about the middle of the nineteenth century, it continued to be frowned upon in the United States. Furthermore, in continental European nations such as France and Germany, cartels abounded and were quite legal. Agreements reached by European cartels could be enforced in the courts, and therefore the agreements worked more satisfactorily there than in America. The long-run result was that small, family-dominated firms tended to survive longer in those countries than in the United States, in part because of the friendlier legal climate for loose associations seeking ways of stabilizing output and prices. Many examples of the modern corporation certainly arose in Europe, especially in Germany, where the financial and political system sometimes encouraged large-scale enterprise. Nevertheless, it is clear that the United States proved a more fertile ground for the spread of big businesses than did early twentieth-century Europe, and the reasons had to do in part with the respective legal frameworks in which business operated.

As Hans B. Thorelli pointed out in his *The Federal Antitrust Policy* (1955), both federal and state law appeared to oppose collusive practices in restraint of trade. Because they were forbidden to engage in cartel behavior, and, more important, because such agreements lacked the force of contracts and could not be enforced in court, American businesses moved more quickly to the genuine formal amalgamation of previously independent companies.

The Congress placed a heavy burden on the courts when it elected to pass such general, vague legislation about concentration. The Supreme Court and lower federal courts struggled with the endless questions that arose about big business and the antitrust law. A price-fixing agreement was obviously illegal, but what were the justices to do when one company legally sold its assets to another? Were such sales illegal if they resulted in restraint or reduction of trade or competition? Was it a matter of degree? How should the effort to create a monopoly be defined? What exactly was a monopoly—100 percent of an industry? 75 percent? 50 percent? Or did that differ with the particular conditions in each industry? If a monopoly or a restraint of trade did exist, how could it be broken up or reversed? Who would organize the new arrangements, and how could they be monitored and evaluated? While the courts continued to wrestle with such conundrums, businesses continued to organize their combinations. If the courts meant to shear the cartel sheep and bypass the integrated-firm goats, it was clearly better to be a goat than a sheep, or at least to look like one. Like the changes in state general incorporation laws, the importance of the Sherman Act was to encourage still further the growing eagerness to try horizontal combinations.

Some scholars have pointed to factors other than the legal environment to explain the big merger wave after 1895. Economist Joe S. Bain, in a contribution to Harold F. Williamson (ed.), *The Growth of the American Economy* (1944), emphasized the importance of the continued growth of the railway system in bringing about vigorous price competition which in turn touched off the merger movement. It is not easy, however, to tie the railroads closely to the merger wave of the turn of the century. Ralph L. Nelson, in his *Merger Movements in American Industry, 1895–1956* (1959), concluded after a careful review of the evidence that there was little causal connection between the additional growth of railroads after about 1880 and the merger wave after 1895. Certainly the creation of a national market and transportation system was a necessary precondition of the explosion of horizontal combinations in the decade from 1895 to 1905, but it is difficult to explain the timing of the flurry of combinations by reference to transportation. It seems clear that a national market had been created at least fifteen years before 1895, and the nation's major cities were already linked by railroads as early as 1860. The great combination movement could surely not have happened without the prior creation of a national transport system, but seems to have lagged somewhat behind that system.

A development more closely linked with unleashing the merger proliferation seems to have been important changes in the nation's investment markets. Advances in transportation and communications had made the modern, large-scale, integrated corporation a possibility. The behavior of prices, profits, and growth rates had started businesses on a long search for cooperative means of controlling their economic environment, and pools and trade associations had proved unsatisfactory. That search for order, as we have seen, began in some industries even before the Civil War, when the early trade associations were formed. Beginning with the Panic of 1873, the hard times of the 1870s caused businesses in many industries to join the search. Throughout the 1870s and 1880s cooperative efforts among manufacturers became common, as they had earlier become on the railroads. Beginning in the late 1880s, changes in the legal setting encouraged and facilitated the transition to the unified firm, and the success of a few highly publicized horizontal combinations had led others in business to think of the possibility of creating similar organizations. Changes in the capital markets removed the last significant institutional barrier and made it much easier to achieve cooperative solutions to competitive problems through mergers. Naomi Lamoreaux's *The Great Merger Movement in American Business, 1895–1904* (1985) argued that the onset of the depression that began with the Panic of 1893 provided the impetus that triggered the tidal wave of mergers at the end of the century. The economic troubles of many manufacturers in that depression led them to seek, as some had been doing for decades, a way out. The resulting rush to mergers both hastened and was hastened by the significant changes in the financial markets.

Before the early 1890s, there was virtually no national market for industrial securities. Except for a few companies, it was not possible for potential investors to buy stock of industrial firms as they so commonly do now. Railroad stocks and bonds accounted for almost all the securities of private businesses available to people in an open market. Industrial stocks were generally considered too risky for this sort of investment, though there was some small-scale trading of industrial shares (such as those of textile companies) on local markets before 1890. There was, however, no national market for "industrials," as they were called. As a result, owners of manufacturing businesses found their capital sunk in their firms and had little opportunity to liquidate their ownership if they wanted to. For example, if a steel mill owner had a quarter-interest in a steel business and wanted to retire from the competitive fray, it was almost impossible to liquidate that interest unless the other owners or a very wealthy outsider wished to buy the quarter-interest. Under those circumstances the owner seeking an exit from the business might possibly have to stay in the firm for lack of a buyer or else might have to settle for less than the interest was really worth in order to find one. If, on the other hand, the unhappy owner held 25,000 of the 100,000 shares in the business, and there was a large, well-established trade in industrial securities, all or part of those shares could then be sold much more easily and probably at a better price. If there were such a securities market, a large number of people could bid for small blocks of the shares and view them simply as investments and not as any real obligation to get into the steel business. Such a market would be a much more accurate and efficient mechanism for evaluating the worth of assets and turning them into cash. In the 1890s such a market arose for the first time, as the securities of industrial corporations gained widespread acceptance among investors and came to be listed on the New York Stock Exchange and traded all over the country and abroad as well. The creation of an industrial securities market made it much easier to build large combinations, and the appearance of more and more successful big businesses helped expand the market for industrials.

The growing attempts to form horizontal combinations produced a ready demand for the funds available from investors in the United States and Europe. By the end of the 1880s a small number of the trust certificates of major horizontal combines had begun to find a market, but only among very speculative investors. Conservative investors would not think of buying such securities because they were considered too risky. By the early 1890s, however, this situation was changing.

During the first years of that decade, as Thomas Navin and Marian Sears showed (*Business History Review*, June 1955), some of the new, large, and apparently legal holding companies began to issue preferred stock, sometimes with the aid of highly reputable bankers. These securities, aided considerably by the growing feeling that the holding companies were on sounder legal ground than the cartel-like trusts, found places on the nation's most important stock exchanges. Many leading investment bankers, including the conservative and very prestigious J. P. Morgan, continued to regard the new industrials with some misgivings, though Morgan himself did help finance one such company—General Electric—in 1893. When the stock market suffered a long downturn in the depression that began in that same year, however, the industrials weathered the storm better than the stocks of most railroads. By the time the economy turned up again in a few years, bankers and investors had gained considerable confidence in industrial securities. In addition, the railroad sector, for decades almost the exclusive focus of trading in stocks, had by the nineties grown tired. The great period of growth by then lay behind the railroads rather than ahead of them, and they had been plagued by financial problems and bankruptcies for years, a situation that was worsened by the depression of the 1890s. The capital markets were increasingly ready to receive large issues of securities from big businesses in manufacturing. When the most gilt-edged banking house of all, J. P. Morgan and Company, underwrote the creation of the Federal Steel Company in 1898, it became clear even to the most cautious of investors in this country and in Europe that it was time to get in on a good thing.

The fact that a solid, brisk market was appearing for industrial securities made it much easier for business leaders to create large combinations. It was considerably less difficult to talk independent manufacturers into giving up their companies to form part of a giant corporation if they could turn their shares into cash in the stock market. In addition, most bankers and promoters who helped work out the financial arrangements by which companies merged saw to it that the new combinations were capitalized at considerably more than the worth of their separate parts (this was the practice many people denounced as "watering" stock). This made it much easier to woo reluctant manufacturers into joining a new combination by offering them shares that might bring more in the stock market than the manufacturers had thought their companies were worth. This suspicious situation was brought about by the fact that the amalgamating firms and promoters found stock market investors ready to buy shares in the new businesses, even at prices considerably higher than the per-share net worth of the corporations. Investors believed in the future growth of the new companies and probably expected good dividends and even higher stock prices in the future. In many cases they got what they expected, but in many less sound cases the results were much more grim. The success of the investments varied greatly, depending on the particular company. The willingness of investors to pay high prices for stocks made it possible for the promoters and underwriters like Morgan to make enormous profits, and for the owners of previously independent concerns to get more than they might have imagined when they joined a combination. The result was that the owners of autonomous businesses found combination increasingly attractive.

Naomi Lamoreaux's *Great Merger Movement* emphasized not only the influence of the depression of the 1890s in heightening price competition and thus encouraging mergers, but also pointed out that particular kinds of industries were especially prone to amalgamation. "Capital-intensive, mass-production industries in which . . . expansion had been rapid on the eve of the Panic of 1893"—industries dominated by relatively new firms—were the most likely ones to seek relief through merger. The impact of mergers was concentrated in such industries.

During the decade after 1895, the great merger movement flourished, and nothing like it was seen before or since in the history of the nation's economy. Approximately 300 separate firms disappeared into mergers each year during that time. By 1910, many of the nation's most influential big businesses had been created either through vertical or horizontal growth, or through a mixture of the two. Just a partial list of modern industrial giants already born by 1910 included: petroleum companies such as Standard Oil and Texaco; rubber producers such as U.S. Rubber and Goodyear; metals firms including U.S. Steel, Bethlehem Steel, American Smelting and Refining, Jones and Laughlin Steel, Anaconda Copper, Phelps-Dodge, International Nickel, and National Lead; the electrical manufacturers General Electric and Westinghouse; food processors such as American Sugar, Nabisco, United Fruit, Swift & Company, and Armour; as well as scores of others including American Tobacco, Du Pont, Pittsburgh Plate Glass, American Can, Allis-Chalmers, International Harvester, Singer, and Eastman Kodak. It is no exaggeration to say that the structure of the modern American economy had been reshaped by the end of the first decade of the twentieth century.

In almost every branch of industry, producers tried to create large-scale businesses. Some, like those mentioned above, were successes. Many, however, were not, as Arthur S. Dewing's *Corporate Promotions and Reorganizations* (1914) showed. Some rose like mushrooms in the night and disappeared almost as quickly. Among the giants that might have been but which failed to achieve long-run success, one could list such unfamiliar firms as American Bicycle, National Starch, U.S. Leather, American Glue, National Salt, National Cordage, Standard Rope & Twine, United Button Company, American Wringer, American Grass Twine, National Novelty, Consolidated Cotton Oil, American Woodworking Machinery, U.S. Dyewood and Extract, American Soda Fountain, National Wallpaper, Mt. Vernon-Woodberry Cotton Duck, and others.

An early, spectacular example of failure was National Cordage. Manufacturers of cordage (rope and twine) tried associations and pools in the 1870s and 1880s which did not bring the stability and security the producers wanted. In 1887 four of the leading companies took the next step, uniting to form the National Cordage Company. In an attempt to gain control of the industry, the cordage combination embarked on an ambitious program of expansion, acquiring additional mills that gave the company nominal control of about forty percent of the country's rope and twine production by 1890. In the summer of that year, the firm's capital stock was increased tenfold to $15,000,000 and still more competitors were brought into the combine. By the early months of 1892, the company effectively controlled approximately ninety percent of the cordage mills in the country. It moved to the forefront of the new industrial giants, enjoying the backing of powerful New York bankers, and the financial press hailed it as a sure success.

Within a single year, however, the mighty cordage trust was on the rocks. Competitors sprang up on every hand and the trust's control of the industry slipped badly. Its financial troubles came to a head in the first week of May, 1893—the firm was unable to pay its obligations, its securities plummeted, and it went bankrupt with breathtaking speed. The nation's leading financial journal summed up the events: "Cordage has collapsed like a bursted meteor."

Another also-ran in the monopoly sweepstakes was the National Salt Company. That firm arose in the giddy days of the great merger wave as a combination of salt producers in New York State in 1899. By parlaying mergers and making imprudent financial arrangements with other producers, the promoters of National Salt secured by 1900 control of about eighty-five to ninety percent of the industry east of the Rockies, according to the company's president. The firm then raised the price of salt. For about a year and half the plan worked well and profits rolled in. The salt trust's fortunes soon suffered a sharp downturn, however, when outsiders rushed into the industry to grab a share of the bonanza. The combine encountered growing difficulty in meeting its financial obligations under the arrangements made earlier to secure its control of the industry. During the course of those troubles, the company defaulted on payments due cooperating salt producers and then tried to escape its obligations by asking the courts to set aside the now troublesome agreements on the grounds that they represented a conspiracy in restraint of trade! The salt barons, it seems, were nothing if not flexible. Even their resourcefulness proved unequal to the task, though, and by 1902 the National Salt Company was in receivership.

Although concentration came to a great many industries, it did not "take" in all of them. Obviously, it was not enough merely to have the unscrupulous and greedy outlook attributed to the "robber barons." Riches were not simply lying on the ground for any would-be monopolists to pick up. What factors explained the ability of some businesses to last while others were quickly cut down and still others disappeared in the wake of later challenges?

A look at the history of concentration in industry in the twentieth-century American economy shows that, in general, the degree of overall concentration and its patterns have not changed greatly since 1910. There were, to be sure, many circumstances and factors that influenced whether a particular firm would become and remain a giant enterprise, including the quality of its management, timing, and luck. But the most important factor in accounting for the rise and persistence of big business has been that giant firms were most likely to appear and to succeed if they were in technologically advanced industries that could achieve and sustain genuine economies of scale and could link mass production to mass distribution. The difficulty and enormous expense of creating new, competitive firms in such industries as steel, nonferrous metals, petroleum, autos, rubber, machinery, electrical manufactures, and chemicals usually either discouraged most outside competitors from venturing into those areas or explained their lack of success if they did enter. The big companies in such industries had by the early twentieth century a very long lead in terms of capital investment in production and distribution networks, managerial talent, scientific or technological expertise (including advantageous patents), and established market positions. Others found it very difficult (though not impossible) to enter and compete successfully with the existing giants. In some industries that involved little in the way of advanced technology, big businesses discouraged competition through heavy advertising and the creation of powerful brand names. Makers of cigarettes and breakfast cereals, for example, raised the cost of introducing new products through massive advertising. Potential competitors were thus discouraged by the very high costs of advertising and of positioning goods in the retail markets, and the market share of the existing large firms was protected. Such costs and risks constituted effective barriers to entry into the industry. In most low-technology industries, however, it was relatively inexpensive for new companies to enter the market, and correspondingly difficult to maintain a high degree of concentration.

The combine in cordage, for example, was a poor gamble from the start. The producers could join together and gain control over prices, but they could not readily maintain that control. It was too easy for others, tempted by the high prices and profits, to enter the industry. The supply of raw materials was abundant, the cost of beginning production was low, and no control was possible at the marketing end of the business. When competitors appeared, the combination could buy them out for a time, but eventually it succumbed to the reestablishment of competition, which destabilized prices and sometimes brought the collapse of the combination. In many industries, then, the workings of market forces insured that society would not be "held up" (at least not for very long) by horizontal combinations. Big business, it was clear, found more fertile soil in some industries than in others.

Even if the entrepreneur were in one of the industries that benefited from the rise of technologies that permitted economies of scale and that could be fitted into a vertically integrated set of economic activities, failure was still possible. The patterns of success, however, are reasonably clear, as detailed in the work of Alfred D. Chandler, Jr. Chandler's analysis is explained most fully in *Scale and Scope* (1990), where he reviews the history of giant enterprises in three of the world's leading industrial economies—the United States, Great Britain, and Germany. In all three nations, Chandler shows, in order to succeed, "entrepreneurs had to make three sets of interrelated investments." They not only had to invest in "production facilities large enough to exploit a technology's potential economies of scale or scope," but they also had to build far-flung marketing and distribution networks, and to recruit and hold an army of managers to administer them, to "monitor and coordinate" production and distribution, and to "plan and allocate resources for future production and distribution." If

they could do all that, *and* if they proved resourceful enough
to react creatively to the threats and the opportunities constantly presented by the changing economic, social, and political environment, they could then sustain their firms' places
in the modern economy.

Although some large firms did appear in low-technology,
unintegrated industries, in general such sectors remained relatively unconcentrated. Examples of the latter included textiles, leather, printing and publishing, lumber and wood, fur-
niture, clothing, most food, and similar industries. Clearly, the
potential empire-builder of the turn of the century would have
done well to choose the right kind of industry in which to seek
and hold the gains enjoyed by the major corporations that
endured long after the merger movement. For those entrepreneurs who were in the new, technologically fertile industries,
however, market constraints were weaker, and society had
much cause for concern about the implications of the advent
of large-scale corporations.

The rise of those giant corporations had produced the
modern American economy in which many important industries were highly concentrated. In those sectors, the appearance
of a few giant companies set new patterns of economic behavior for business.

The new big businesses called forth profound worries
about the danger of corporate power in an emerging economic
order that was fundamentally different from the old, classically
competitive one. The old days of small firms and the kind of
competition most economists still talk about—the "Golden
Age of Competition," Alfred Eichner called it—were gone for-
ever in many important industries. In their search for stability,
order, and steady profits, business leaders had eventually created large, integrated, unified firms that, along with a few similar companies, often formed concentrated or oligopolistic industries. These new businesses, unlike the older, smaller ones,
seldom competed by offering prices appreciably lower than
those of their major rivals. Price competition, they had
learned, could be reduced by businesses so big that their output

formed a significant enough share of the market to influence the pricing of others. In the older economy, the number of producers was usually so large and the size of each so small that one manufacturer could usually cut prices without affecting the output and price decisions of the many other firms in that particular line of business. Such behavior under the new conditions of oligopoly and high fixed costs, however, often led to the falling prices that had first led businesses down the road to combination. Instead, much of the economy moved into a new era of "administered" prices. Sometimes, as in the case of the steel industry, the largest firm would exercise what came to be called "price leadership." Under that system, the other big producers would simply follow the lead of the major company. Outright price-fixing through collusion became relatively rare, not only because it continued to be illegal, but also because it was not really necessary. The major producers, now armed with improved cost accounting, all knew their costs, and they had a pretty good idea of their competitors' costs. Therefore it was relatively easy to arrive at a sort of "standard" industry price which everyone tacitly agreed to maintain and which greatly improved the chances for a good return on the capital invested in the enterprises.

Instead of competing in price, the oligopolists learned to compete in other, less crude ways. These included different methods of sales promotion (mass media advertising, for example) and different quality or alleged quality in goods and services. The new competition meant constant striving for the most efficient systems of organization for production and distribution, and a never-ending effort to plan, to react to changing circumstances, and to allocate resources so as to keep the enterprise growing via new products and services. The modern corporation, rather than Adam Smith's classical and invisible market forces, came to be the means through which modern economic life was ordered. This great watershed in the history of business was summed up in Alfred Chandler's title for his 1977 book, *The Visible Hand: The Managerial Revolution in American Business.*

Later, those managing the corporations would figure out additional ways to protect or improve their share of the market, such as introducing concepts of planned obsolescence, the "latest style," and other mechanisms through which the psychological needs of consumers would be influenced and satisfied. In some cases, such as the automobile industry, the older ideas of products as utilitarian objects was replaced by the notion of products as symbols of status, sex appeal, and material achievement. Subtle (and sometimes not so subtle) appeals to pride, prejudice, fear, and the endless varieties of human desire often replaced the older, nineteenth-century appeals to what consumers wanted then (or were thought to want)—thrift, utility, and durability. The new forms of competition were part of a radically different economic and social environment. As Arthur R. Burns noted in his book *The Decline of Competition* (1936), "the rise of the 'heavy industries,' changes in methods of selling, and the widening use of the corporate forms of business organization are bringing, if they have not already brought, the era of competitive capitalism to a close." A brave new world of oligopolies, administered prices, competition on grounds other than price, and relatively stable market shares had replaced the older kind of competition. A great many Americans wondered whether the nation was better or worse off.

CHAPTER THREE

Corporate Triumph: "Capitalistic, Centralizing, and Mechanical"

During any period of rapid, widespread upheaval in society, people undergo enormous stress and tension as the old ways yield to the new. Sometimes the resulting shifts in power and opinion even touch off violent, radical reactions. Most often, however, society simply gropes its way to a gradual acceptance of change, and a new brand of social equilibrium emerges. The rise of big business and the triumph of industrial civilization certainly constituted a massive social change during the years bracketed by the Civil War and World War I. The upheaval was great, and for many the acceptance of the rising corporate order was painful indeed. "Such great revolutions," Henry Adams noted in his autobiography in 1905, "commonly leave some bitterness behind." As the twentieth century passed, however, it would become clear that not only was big business here to stay, it was here to conquer all before it. Big business proved to be the seedbed of a new social and economic order. The new managerial class, governed by the engineering values of efficiency and systematic approaches to problems, having

first arisen to help create and then to serve the modern corporation, soon became the dominant element in an urban and
then suburban civilization. Other segments of the great middle
class quickly found in big business a complex and comprehensive set of organizing values; soon almost the entire society
would come to be influenced by corporate ways of doing things.
This did not happen universally or instantly, to be sure, but
the corporation would establish its hegemony with relative
speed and become the dominant institution in American life.
The triumph of the corporation as the most powerful element
in American society worked on many levels, affecting politics
most immediately, but reshaping labor as well, and signaling
the enshrinement of technology and science as the new American gods. In time the corporation would restructure much of
society according to its own image, not only in the United
States but throughout the developed world. Most of those developments, however, would become wholly clear only with
the passage of time. As the nineteenth century drew to a close,
the issues seemed very much in doubt.

Uncertainty and unease about the emerging order of corporations and "trusts" took many forms. The nation's farmers
found themselves increasingly subject to the fluctuations of a
national and often international market for their produce, a
set of complex economic factors they did not always understand. When their problems began to grow, agrarians tended
to blame them on the murky dealings of railroad executives,
eastern bankers, industrialists, crooked politicians, and other
sinister individuals. Agrarian protest began shortly after the
close of the Civil War with the Patrons of Husbandry, better
known to history as the Grangers. They were soon supplanted
by agrarian political pressure organizations called farmers' alliances, whose successes in electing candidates to state and
federal offices in the 1880s led them to form a national party
in 1892. Joining with dissident workers and with other groups,
the farmers spawned the Populist Party, declaring in their famous Omaha platform of 1892 that "a vast conspiracy against

mankind" was underway and that a populist crusade would have to be waged to crush it.

During the last three decades of the nineteenth century, a varied array of protest groups voiced their unhappiness. A small minority of the nation's workers joined to create viable unions, first in the form of broad-gauged, reform-oriented institutions like the National Labor Union and the Knights of Labor. Those organizations tried to appeal to all segments of working people, and they sought to overturn the wage system and produce goods through cooperative enterprises. Eventually such groups merged with the populists in the 1890s. In addition to the farmers and workers who called for fundamental change, another reform impulse of the period focused on the rather confused fight to alter the currency. A succession of political parties and interest groups from the Greenbackers through the advocates of the increased issue of silver coinage all sought to solve society's problems through inflation. Others attacked different aspects of the national discontent. The followers of Henry George worked for a more nearly equal distribution of wealth through taxing privately owned land, which they believed to be the key to reversing the exploitation of the people. Many of these reform groups coalesced in the 1890s in the Populist Party and (in 1896) gained control of the national Democratic Party. They then sought to concentrate their efforts on the silver issue in the famous contest for the presidency between William Jennings Bryan and William McKinley. Bryan's crushing defeat in that election demoralized the agrarian crusade, and that fact, perhaps along with the return of prosperity to the farm belt, resulted in the retreat of most farmers from the reform cause. Following the prescription of Kansas populist Mary Ellen Lease, they had raised less corn and more hell, until the price of corn rose.

The progressive movement then took up the cause, continuing to criticize railroads, giant manufacturing concerns, and influential bankers. The progressives mixed efforts to improve the democratic process (via secret ballots, direct election of Senators, the use of city managers rather than elected mayors, and so on) with attempts to control or attack businesses, as well as with some changes which the representatives of big business also favored, such as the creation of the Federal Reserve System. Theodore Roosevelt gained a reputation as a "trust buster" by having his Justice Department prosecute several widely hated corporations, and Woodrow Wilson won the White House in 1912, running as an opponent of big business.

The reform movements have all been chronicled and analyzed in considerable detail by generations of historians, and there is little point in recounting the story here. For our purposes, however, we may overlook the intricacies of the historical treatment of the politics and motivations of the reform movements and look instead at some of the basic political and economic issues raised by the coming of big business. We will also touch briefly on some of the multiple meanings of the rise of the modern corporation for American life outside the explicitly political realm.

Perhaps the broadest, most diffuse issue that troubled Americans during the fifty years or so discussed in this book was the fear that the new economic order was destroying America's status as a land of opportunity. Citizens in many walks of life found the revolution in business disturbing and worrisome for that reason. Often persons who enlisted in the fight against big business were those whose jobs or social standing had been affected adversely, such as the wholesalers who found giant corporations taking over the marketing of more and more goods in the changing economy. Those in small businesses driven into bankruptcy or forced to sell out to a combination voiced angry resentment. The ranks of progressivism swelled with people who had thrived in the older economy, but whose businesses or livelihoods had little or no place in the world of oligopolies and integrated firms. Much of the unhappiness of such people was rooted in their middle-class vision of what America was supposed to be. The ideal of the opportunity for all citizens to acquire and operate their own businesses died hard. The fascination with the goal of making "each man his own boss" extended throughout much of American society.

As big business expanded its dominion over much of the economy, more and more people came to realize that they would have to sacrifice the hope of going into business for themselves and accept the idea of going to work for a large organization. Most would accept it in time, and many would even come to see virtue in the idea of moving up within the corporate world, but for millions it was a bitter pill.

Some of these basic attitudes were touched upon by critics of big business who testified before the U.S. Industrial Commission, a turn-of-the-century governmental body set up to investigate the problem of growing concentration in industry. Mr. P. E. Dowe, the representative of an association of traveling salesmen (a group hard hit by corporate integration into marketing), voiced the American Dream of the Gilded Age: "Every commercial traveler hopes to attain, both as the goal of the ambitious and progressive businessman and as an equitable return for years of hard work under trying conditions, a business of his own or in conjunction with others." Recalling the traveling men who had been forced to go to work for huge combinations and thus to give up their independence, Dowe noted the passing of the old order and conjured up a bleak vision of the future. "The history of this country," he declared, "gives examples of poor boys who became great men, beginning at splitting rails, tanning hides, driving canal horses, etc., and we all know personally some illustration of self-made men; we have listened to the stories of father and grandsire, telling the younger generation of early struggles, and many instances have been cited where a few hundred or a few thousand dollars started them upon a career to fame and fortune. Trusts have come, however, as a curse for this generation and a barrier to individual enterprise. What will be the prospects for our children? God-Almighty alone knows." This fear of the effects of big business upon individualism and the cherished prospect of people to achieve upward mobility lay at the heart of the widespread unease about the emergence of the corporate world. Like the so-called "closing of the frontier" announced in the 1890s by historian Frederick Jackson Turner, the coming of giant corporations seemed to signal the end of an open, promising America and the beginning of a land of diminished opportunity. Americans who grew up on the philosophy of Ben Franklin and the dream of the self-made man were troubled by the new visions of success embodied in climbing corporate ladders and moving up organization charts.

Another disturbing aspect of the rise of big business was the ruthless and sometimes unscrupulous use of economic power by men like John D. Rockefeller and James Duke in order to crush their rivals. People objected to such unfair competitive practices as allowing secret rebates, waging selective price wars to drive competitors into bankruptcy and forcing them to sell out at bargain prices, refusing to supply wholesalers unless they agreed to market only the supplier's products, and the like. Critics of business lambasted these practices, and it is clear that most Americans agreed then and probably still agree that such behavior is unethical, antisocial, and a misuse of economic power. Initially, the nation tried to solve this difficulty by passing laws that specifically forbade the use of particular economic tactics. The railroad regulatory laws, for example, made illegal the use of rebates and different rates for the same classes of shippers. In manufacturing, the issue of unfair competitive practices involved primarily discriminatory behavior. A firm large enough to constitute a significant portion of an industry used the power inherent in its size to secure favorable treatment in the purchase of raw materials, in the transportation of goods, raw materials, or personnel, or in the marketing of products. Often the favorable treatment was deserved because it was economically and socially advantageous (that is, it often reflected genuine savings in bulk buying, transport, and mass merchandising), but sometimes it was not (as in the case of the rebates demanded by big shippers and denied to others making similar but less frequent shipments). Whenever other competitors could not secure equal treatment for equivalent business activities, unfair advantages accrued to the largest firms.

In time, however, it became clear that the nation's law-makers could not outlaw specific practices as fast as inventive businesses could come up with new ones. As a result, it became the nation's policy to create regulatory agencies with broad general powers to oversee and discipline the competitive behavior of big businesses. Under the administration of Theodore Roosevelt, the U.S. Bureau of Corporations was set up as an agency to investigate and publicize the unethical competitive methods of offending businesses. The notion that publicity about business's doings would cause it to behave better was as old as the problem of big business itself and had been at the heart of the first wave of state railroad regulatory bodies, the "sunshine commissions." It quickly became apparent that this idea was too optimistic, and Roosevelt soon proposed a stronger regulatory body. In 1914, this body came into being in the form of the Federal Trade Commission, an agency armed with some enforcement powers, as well as with the right to investigate and publicize business activity. As it had done earlier with the railroads, the nation tried to insure fair behavior in big business by creating a regulatory commission to oversee and police the activities of private firms, but not to determine some specific degree of concentration in industry. The evolution of the antitrust laws came to mean much the same thing. In its landmark 1911 decision in the Standard Oil case, the Supreme Court announced the so-called "rule of reason," which made a distinction between good and bad trusts, though the justices did not use those terms. Giant companies that operated fairly and did not use objectionable competitive methods, the high court indicated, would not be judged guilty of violating the antitrust legislation. The judiciary would not attack any firm on the basis of its size alone, but rather on the basis of its behavior.

The result of those developments was the creation of a new role for the national government in the economy as watchdog of the private sector, a basically negative, policing role. The combined efforts of the regulatory agencies, the Justice Department, and the courts were supposed to prevent the worst sorts of discriminatory use of economic power. In time, as Thomas K. McCraw's *Prophets of Regulation* (1984) made clear, regulation would take many, sometimes contradictory forms, some aimed merely at disclosure and publicity, some opposed to monopoly, and still others having the effect of protecting and cartelizing powerful interests. The beginnings of regulation did clearly demonstrate that, in the face of the rise of giant corporations, the nation had made the political decision that the affairs of businesses (previously largely private) were subject to public scrutiny. The competitive behavior of business would therefore permanently become a legitimate concern of government. In essence, regulation became, as McCraw concluded, an ever-changing series of political settlements "undertaken in an effort to keep peace within the polity." It made as much sense as such settlements customarily do, and it represented a compromise, a painful acceptance of the corporate world.

Americans had come in the end to believe that big business was all but inevitable, that the new world of complex organizations, bureaucracy, and giant enterprise had permanently transformed their civilization. Some critics would continue to argue, as Woodrow Wilson did in the 1912 presidential campaign, that if only firms could be made to give up their unfair practices, the old system of smaller, more competitive companies would reemerge. The immoral, underhanded doings of the robber barons, this theory held, had prevented the normal workings of the competitive marketplace. Conspiracy and greed, many would prefer to believe, explained the rise of large-scale enterprises. As we have seen, however, relatively few companies owed their power primarily to the use of such tactics. The dynamics of industrial capitalism, as Alfred Chandler's work has established, rested on much deeper and more substantial foundations. It surely was true that Andrew Carnegie, John D. Rockefeller, James Duke, and other "robber barons" were hard men—unyielding, ruthless, and willing to utilize every bit of economic muscle at their command to protect and enlarge their empires. The economic power they used so coldly, however, was usually based on their ability to marshall resources effectively on a huge scale, to create new goods and services, and to produce and distribute them more efficiently and cheaply than could much smaller companies. Rockefeller's dominion over oil ultimately rested on the fact that his costs were the lowest in the industry. The long-term success of Carnegie Steel was similarly based on its greater efficiency in production and distribution, not just on enormous greed or greater ruthlessness. Society could tell such business leaders to stop using rebates or other forms of arm-twisting, and the message could be strong enough to lessen their control or influence somewhat, but would definitely not be strong enough to restore the fabled "Golden Age of Competition." Bigness, in short, would not go away once unfair methods of competition were restrained. What then? Was the government to tear down Carnegie's mills and Rockefeller's refineries? Such notions had little appeal to serious people witnessing their country's emergence as the world's leading industrial nation. Instead, throughout society, the triumph of the corporation and its ways began to reshape modern America. In the political sphere, as we have seen, big business would be accepted and the polity would put in place its own versions of the corporation's bureaucracies, rules, systems, managers, engineers, and lawyers.

The patrician Henry Adams, one of the most thoughtful Americans of his or any generation, summed it up well in *The Education of Henry Adams*, written in 1905. "For a hundred years," he wrote, "the American people had hesitated, vacillated, swayed forward and back, between two forces, one simply industrial, the other capitalistic, centralizing, and mechanical." The rejection of the populist crusade in 1896 was for Adams the decisive moment. After that it was clear that "a capitalistic system had been adopted, and if it were to be run at all, it must be run by capital and by capitalistic methods; for nothing could surpass the nonsensity of trying to run so complex and so concentrated a machine by Southern and Western farmers in grotesque alliance with city day-laborers."

"Once admitted that the machine must be efficient," he concluded in resignation, "society might dispute in what social interest it should be run, but in any case it must work concentration." It would bring concentration not only in the political sphere but in other realms of American life as well.

One of those areas transformed by the coming of big business and the corporate world was the relationship between labor and management. The triumph of the corporation also changed, though not so deeply, the nature of work itself. The rise of the factory system and industrialization, it must be remembered, came before the creation of modern, large-scale enterprises. It was the industrial revolution that first brought the technological advances associated with the ever greater use of machines in production and the growing division of labor. The spread of machines, the factory, and the breaking down of complex jobs that previously had been done by one person into a series of simpler, more specialized, but more repetitive, boring, and unchallenging tasks—were all developments that preceded big business. (Adam Smith himself had rhapsodized about the productivity increases that could come from the division of labor in the famous pin-factory examples in *The Wealth of Nations*, published the year the American Revolution broke out.) Capitalists introduced the new technologies of the industrial revolution both to capture increases in productivity and to strengthen their hands against their powerful skilled workers. Mechanization of production almost always meant a loss of power and status among skilled workers, whose scarce talents had given them real leverage against their employers and had always made them the heart of the nation's labor union movement.

The spread of the division of labor and of mechanization led to what many historians have called "deskilling," or the building of production skills into the machines and processes rather than the reliance on skilled workers. In industry after industry in the nineteenth century, the proliferation of mechanization brought discontent among the existing workforce, resistance by the elite skilled workers, strikes, and labor unrest.

The transformation of some skilled work into a more dehumanizing experience, with workers subjected to boring, repetitive tasks, was a part of industrialization itself. The introduction of deskilling also brought the beginnings of a long struggle over who would control shop-floor working conditions, the skilled workers or the bosses. Each time there was a significant change in the production process, a new machine or a new arrangement of machines, rancorous questions were raised about who would decide how work would be done, in what sequence, and on what schedule. These conflicts, along with tensions brought by wage cuts in economic downturns, led to many of the strikes and the violence that broke out from time to time in industrial settings. The resistance of skilled workers, unions, strikes, and violent confrontations were always the exception rather than the rule in the overall history of labor in the United States, but they were highly visible and deeply troubling signs of the stresses associated with the changing nature of work in an industrialized society. Such confrontations added considerably, as we have seen, to the political conflicts of the nineteenth century. They were a sharp reminder that technological and industrial "progress" carried real costs as well as benefits. Conflicts such as those of the destructive railroad strikes of 1877, the Haymarket riot, and the strikes at Homestead and at Pullman contributed strongly to the widespread sense of unease about the direction in which the nation seemed to be moving. The coming of big business substantially heightened those anxieties, though the transformation that the corporation brought to the nature of work involved changes in degree rather than changes in kind.

The machine, the factory, mass production, deskilling, and alienation were all plainly evident even before the pioneering industrial corporations appeared in the 1880s, but the new technologies that propelled so many of the early big businesses did mean the extension and expansion of the changes that made workers feel like insignificant cogs in giant, impersonal wheels. A new scale, complexity, and an extreme subdivision of labor were associated with many of the technologies of mass production, continuous processing, and integrated production and distribution systems in the industries that made and marketed such things as farm machinery, electrical manufactures, tobacco products, refined petroleum, metals, sewing machines, flour, sugar, telephones, chemicals, and, especially, automobiles. It was the automobile industry, and above all the company that would dominate that industry in its early stages—Ford—that would in time come to stand for the worst in the dehumanization of work that began with the rise of the factory system. Henry Ford had introduced the car for the masses, the revolutionary Model T, in 1908. In 1910 he opened his huge plant in Highland Park, Michigan, the site that quickly came to symbolize for many the evils of unrestrained mass production. Within a few short years of its opening Highland Park had become the birthplace of and the showcase for full-blown assembly line production. That technology, perhaps more than any other, illustrated the extent to which the worker had become little more than an appendage to an enormous and ominous mechanical system. (Such concerns would inspire Charlie Chaplin's classic 1936 indictment of mass production, "Modern Times.") In many of the mass production industries of the late nineteenth and early twentieth centuries, there was a relative shrinkage of both skilled and unskilled jobs. Instead, more workers fell into a category of people who could be quickly trained (and readily replaced) in highly mechanized factories, refineries, processing plants, and distribution centers. More and more frequently, commentators spoke not of the skilled and the unskilled but of the "semi-skilled." More troubling was the fact that they also spoke of the rise of the "machine-tenders." The long journey begun in Adam Smith's pin factory had led ultimately to Highland Park. For millions of Americans, work itself had become, in Henry Adams's phrase, capitalistic, centralizing, and mechanical.

Although the nature of work was altered by the rise of big business, the coming of the corporation meant even more fundamental changes in the relationships between labor and management outside the realm of the shop floor. The factory system found its first implementation in the textile industry, but by the 1880s it had spread, as Carroll D. Wright noted in his 1883 essay for the tenth federal census of manufactures, to the making of "boots and shoes, of watches, musical instruments, clothing, agricultural implements, metallic goods generally, firearms, carriages and wagons, wooden goods, rubber goods, and even the slaughtering of hogs." Daniel M. Nelson, in *Managers and Workers: Origins of the New Factory System in the United States 1880–1920* (1975), characterized the factory as the foreman's empire. Although owners often visited their factories and sometimes took a hands-on posture, much of the real power rested with the foreman. "Hiring and firing, assignment to tasks, setting the pay rate (by day or by piece), determining who got laid off or told to stay overtime, and resolving disputes all lay in the foreman's domain," wrote David Montgomery in *The Fall of the House of Labor: The Workplace, the State, and American Labor Activism, 1865–1925* (1987). "A foreman could favor those he liked with day rates, generous piece rates, relatively easy or pleasant tasks, permission to miss work to tend sick children or visit aged parents, and early recall from seasonal shutdowns." In some highly skilled work environments, foremen were rare, and decisions about shop-floor operations were handled by senior skilled craftsmen. In both situations, owners and what we would today think of as managers played a minor role in basic production decisions. Turnover was high, workers (especially the less skilled) moved frequently from place to place and job to job, periods of unemployment were common, the firm's labor force usually was relatively small, and the treatment of workers was, by later standards, harsh. The term often applied to work relations in this era—the "drive system"—says much about the climate on the job. There was virtually no job security and very little in the way of benefits beyond the day's or the week's wage. There was little notion of the "rights of labor." David Brody, in *Steelworkers in America: The Nonunion Era* (1960), quoted a manufacturer's views on the subject: "If a man is dissatisfied, it is his privilege to quit." As the factory system spread, some factories becoming huge installations, and multiplant operations beginning to appear, the instability, informality, arbitrariness, and variability in the relations between labor and management was highlighted. In both the emerging mass production industries and the older industries with smaller production runs—those characterized by what Philip Scranton called "flexible production" in his two books, *Proprietary Capitalism* (1983) and *Figured Tapestry* (1989)—efforts emerged to impose more order on the chaos of labor relations. From two separate strands there would be woven together in the modern corporation a new set of much more standardized relationships between management and labor. One of those strands was industrial engineering, often known simply as Taylorism; the other was the employee-benefit schemes called "welfare work." Eventually these practices would unite under the domain of the personnel department, later renamed the "human resource" department by its professional practitioners.

It was the engineers who first discovered and analyzed the lack of systematic practices in production arrangements. The engineering profession was virtually nonexistent before the great era of canal and railroad construction, and by 1850 there were still only 2,000 civil engineers in the United States. "The rising demand for engineers by industry," wrote Edwin Layton in *The Revolt of the Engineers* (1971), touched off explosive growth in that profession. "The golden age for the application of science to American industry came from 1880 to 1920," Layton noted, "a period which also witnessed the rise of large industrial corporations. In these forty years, the engineering profession increased by almost 2,000 percent, from 7,000 to 136,000 members." From the engineers there came a thoroughgoing critique of factory management. Beginning in the 1870s, industrial engineers and manufacturers including Henry R. Towne, Henry Metcalfe, and Frederick A. Halsey pioneered what came to be known as the systematic management movement. A variety of engineering journals, such as the *Trans-*

actions of the American Society of Mechanical Engineers, Engineering Magazine, and (later) *System,* published the literature of what Joseph Litterer termed (in a 1963 article in the *Business History Review*) "the beginnings of a management technology." Managers, these critics pointed out, had almost no control over their production systems under the chaotic regime of the factory system and mass production technologies of the late nineteenth century. Distanced from an increasingly complex, subdivided, and nonintegrated production system, managers had yielded too much control to foremen and to skilled workers. As a result, the industrial engineers argued, the firms had suffered what Litterer called "organizational uncoupling." The solution was "systematic management," which included massive efforts to learn what the foremen and the craft workers knew of their jobs, to place in management's heads and hands that knowledge of how the jobs were actually done, and if possible to streamline and improve the processes of work. Analysis and understanding had to begin with detailed data. Therefore management set out to record information on the materials and work involved in each step of the production process, to try to match output with demand better than in the past, to control inventories, to install cost accounting procedures, and to put in place new ways of paying workers, including refinements to existing piece-rate and wage systems, as well as some pioneering efforts at profit sharing. Jobs were broken down into many subjobs, often into dozens of individual, minute tasks, to be coordinated by managers using data gathered on the jobs and on the production needs of the firm. As Litterer notes, there were two unifying elements in these varied efforts, "a careful definition of duties and responsibilities coupled with standardized ways of performing these duties" and "a specific way of gathering, handling, analyzing, and transmitting information." All this was aimed at establishing managerial control over the production process, from which it had become disconnected. This directly threatened the independence and shop-floor power of both the foreman and the highly skilled worker.

The work of the industrial engineers who argued for systematic management at first received little attention outside a small circle of professional engineers and managers. Soon, however, this idea moved into the public consciousness through the missionary work of the man who came to symbolize industrial engineering, Frederick W. Taylor. Taylor was a zealous advocate for the new approach to the management of production, and under his leadership systematic management became better known as scientific management. From about 1895 until his death in 1915, Taylor publicized his ideas vigorously, and on the whole they met with an enthusiastic and favorable reception. Under his leadership the movement took on the overtones of a great crusade. Taylor was the messiah, and his close followers were often referred to as disciples. He offered to troubled business leaders what he called a solution to "the labor problem." Taylor believed that workers responded to only one incentive, money, and that many were naturally prone to do less work than they could. His ideas about organizing work were developed over many years, during the course of his work at several manufacturing operations, primarily in the metalworking industry. The Taylor system began with the conviction that each worker's particular abilities could be scientifically determined, and every job could be likewise tested to determine a standard day's output from a "first-class worker." The trick then was to assign the right employees to the right jobs. The testing of workers and of jobs involved the stopwatches and the time-and-motion studies that soon came to symbolize Taylorism in the public mind. This kind of testing reinforced the seemingly scientific, clinical, objective air of this new, secular religion. So did the complex array of pay schemes. Once those appropriate Taylorite pay incentives were put into place to reward the workers, went the theory, the employees would cheerfully respond with increased productivity. Additional elements in the Taylor doctrine included large planning departments to coordinate and monitor each detail in the production process, hosts of "functional foremen" to replace the generalist foremen, and refined pay schemes to reward industrious employees. Everyone—employees, bosses, owners, and society in general—would be happier and better off. Here was en elixir for a troubled age.

In a short time Taylorism became famous far and wide as the embodiment of the era's love affair with the idea of efficiency. It seemed to offer a means of restructuring the work environment so as to remove or reduce conflict, improve efficiency, and increase satisfaction by evaluating proficiency on a scientific basis. The stresses and strains of recurrent class conflict could be gotten around by treating everyone objectively and dispassionately. As Samuel Haber pointed out in *Efficiency and Uplift: Scientific Management in the Progressive Era, 1890-1920* (1964), Taylorism allowed the progressives to retain their almost mystical (and elitist) belief in the power of experts while at the same time keeping faith with democratic ideals. Its proponents ranged across the political spectrum and throughout the world. Taylor's admirers even came to include Lenin, who thought that scientific management would fit well with the "scientific socialism" being crafted in the young Soviet Union. Its usefulness seemed to know no bounds, and every sphere from government to forest management and even surgery and baseball were thought to be susceptible to improvement through the application of the Taylorite principles of objective efficiency. Throughout Europe, as Thomas Hughes noted in *American Genesis: A Century of Invention and Technological Enthusiasm, 1870-1970* (1989), the essence of the genius and the explosive energies of an America emerging as a model for the industrial world in the twentieth century were thought to be bound up in a combination of Taylorism and Fordism. Scientific management and Ford's production system perfected at Highland Park were thought to be the twin beacons offered by the New World to the Old. As a German phrase of the time stated it, Taylorism plus Fordism equalled Americanism.

Taylorism was in fact not scientific or objective at all, embodying as it did a host of hidden arbitrary assumptions and subjective judgments about jobs and about the people who

do them. When Taylor and his disciples were hired by industrialists eager to receive the panacea, what happened in the
plants and the offices often was far from what was promised.
As Daniel Nelson's *Managers and Workers* has shown, scientific management in any genuine and thorough form was in
fact introduced in only a relative handful of plants, and even
then not very successfully. It certainly offered no solution to
labor-management conflicts, and it was often opposed by middle managers as well as by workers. Nevertheless it had a wide
impact in shaping the thinking of generations of engineers and
managers on the topic of labor-management relations. Its
harsh, mechanistic, and materialistic view of human beings in
the workplace was soon softened, however, by a process in
which it was melded with a very different set of practices
known as welfare work.

Many middle-class reformers and a fair number of "en-
lightened" business leaders came to believe that the problems
of labor unrest, turnover, and associated social conflicts could
best be addressed not through scientific management but
through a series of efforts to humanize the corporation and
the workplace. This revived an old theme in the history of
industrialization, going back to the paternalistic environments
of early mill villages and model factory towns such as Lowell,
Massachusetts. In the manner of the age, however, the new
movement was to be systematic, rational, and efficient.

Employers soon came to experiment with a variety of
ways to make life better for the workers both on and off the
job by providing an array of educational, recreational, and
generally uplifting activities and facilities. These included
clean, well-lighted lunchrooms, cafeterias, washrooms, librar-
ies, club houses, YMCAs and YWCAs, sports teams and play-
ing fields, company picnics, factory landscaping, and sometimes extensive company housing or whole idealized towns
such as the one the Pullman Company built near Chicago.
Many firms hired specialists, usually called welfare secretaries,
to give direction and impetus to such activities. These specialists were often women with backgrounds in social work,

committed to a middle-class vision of an improved and uplifted workforce shaped by the benevolent hand of the caring corporation. Widespread efforts to launch modest pension and profit sharing plans also marked the era's efforts to build up a feeling of shared interest between the corporation and its employees. Firms such as H. J. Heinz, Pullman, the Filene's department store in Boston, and the National Cash Register Company led the way. The cause was also vigorously promoted by such prominent civic organizations as the League for Social Service and the National Civic Federation. Soon they were joined by universities, which began to offer training courses in welfare practices, and by many in government, as Stuart Brandes noted in his disapproving study, *American Welfare Capitalism, 1880–1940* (1976). In the view of the proponents of welfarism, workers were influenced by far more than the narrow monetary concerns Taylor saw; to improve work and life in an industrial and corporate society, it was necessary to uplift the minds, shape the values, and improve the work, home, and community environments of America's workers and their families.

The movement attracted much attention and support in the business community. Daniel Nelson reported in *Managers and Workers* that "before World War I," at least forty manufacturing firms had "introduced extensive welfare programs" and that "hundreds ... adopted more modest programs." In a related effort, business and the educational system joined forces to promote vocational training programs in the schools, yet another middle-class effort to shape the working class for more productive and happier lives in the emerging corporate order. The millions of new immigrants from eastern and southern Europe, in particular, were the intended beneficiaries of such training and education. In his 1985 study, *Employing Bureaucracy*, Sanford M. Jacoby points out that "proponents of industrial education argued that tighter links between the schools and the economy would enable the nation to cope more effectively with the stresses and strains of becoming an industrial urban society." Along with the stronger influences of scientific management and welfare work, the vocational guidance movement would prove to be one of the streams that joined to produce, by about 1920, the new profession of personnel management. Henceforward, according to the most progressive thinking of the day, the chaos and conflict between management and labor would be mitigated. Bureaucracy, order, and efficiency had found a human face: the caring corporation—one big family, supporting a progressive social order in which all could seek improvement and their proper places. Soon there would be, under the aegis of the ubiquitous corporate personnel departments, more uniform systems of hiring, promoting, firing, caring for, and disciplining an increasingly white collar workforce. Millions of middle-level managers, supervisors, clerks, and operatives would all share relatively similar values and experiences within the world of the corporation, experiencing what Olivier Zunz referred to in *Making America Corporate, 1870–1920* (1990) as "a homogeneous work culture." The old order was giving way to the new, corporate order.

In a limited fashion, the coming of the corporation also offered new opportunities to women in the workforce, though equality of opportunity and of experience at work remained only a dream. The best-known example of change in this area is perhaps the opening of clerical jobs in the office, analyzed in Margery W. Davies, *Woman's Place Is at the Typewriter: Office Work and Office Workers, 1870–1930* (1982). Responding to the pressures of rapid growth in office staffs, corporations provided some jobs for women in what had traditionally been male occupations. Responding to a variety of economic and social pressures, women themselves sought both clerical and professional employment more aggressively than before. Change came not only to the office but to the factory as well. "In the factory," wrote Alice Kessler-Harris in *Out to Work: A History of Wage-Earning Women in the United States* (1982), "newly developed techniques such as welfare programs, personnel offices, and scientific management reduced some of the barriers to hiring women." These changes, how-

ever, were relatively modest, though more significant ones lay
in the decades ahead.

The growing influence of the corporation soon touched
other elements in American life as well. By the early twentieth
century many of the big businesses in the high-technology,
science-based industries such as the electrical manufacturers,
communications companies, machinery producers, and chem-
ical firms had forged strong ties to the institutions of science
and technology. Some added to their array of corporate skills
and missions the research and development of new products
and processes, leading the way to one of the twentieth century's
primary engines of economic growth, formal departments of
research and development (R&D). The pioneering firms included ones that would remain at the forefront of the application of R&D for decades to come—General Electric, AT&T,
Du Pont, Eastman Kodak, and others. Although Thomas Edison and his Menlo Park "invention factory" were the popular
symbols of this aspect of big business, it was in fact some of
the early German enterprises such as Bayer and BASF that
provided the real models for the American corporate leaders
in the organized teamwork of research and development, as
David A. Hounshell and John Kenley Smith, Jr. argued in
Science and Corporate Strategy: Du Pont R&D, 1902–1980
(1988). (These same firms were also among the leaders in the
European versions of welfare work.) Hounshell and Smith
quote Arthur D. Little's 1913 observation that "Germany has
long been recognized as preeminently the country of organized
research" and point out that "many of the U.S. pioneers, including Du Pont, took their cues from developments in Germany." Two of America's first universities oriented primarily
toward research and graduate education, Johns Hopkins and
Clark, were also based on German models, and so were the
research and graduate studies programs emerging at such universities as Harvard, Clark, Columbia, Chicago, and Wiscon-
sin, according to David Noble's *America by Design: Science,
Technology, and the Rise of Corporate Capitalism* (1977).

Noble's work details and analyzes the intimate connections that arose early in the twentieth century among the corporations, the science and engineering establishments, and the universities. The creation of the first true research and development laboratory in the United States, that of General Electric, was emblematic of the web of connections that quickly tied the modern corporation to the modern university. At the opening of the twentieth century GE hired to head its R&D operation Willis R. Whitney, a professor of chemistry at MIT (Massachusetts Institute of Technology); by 1906 Whitney's department included more than 100 employees, many of whom were drawn, like himself, from the university world. All the big businesses that had major stakes in science and engineering came to have strong, ongoing relationships with leading research universities, recruiting staff and consultants in ever-growing numbers as the century progressed. Anyone who has attended or taught at an American university understands the ties between departments of science and engineering and the corporate community. Their interaction and interdependence played a leading role in shaping research both within the academic and the corporate settings. The needs, values, and priorities of big business came to influence the entire realm of institutions of higher learning. In a similar way, the vocational training movement in particular and the secondary education system in general were designed in part to respond to the corporation's requirements for employees able to meet the daily needs of modern businesses. Education serves many purposes in our society, but none has been thought so vital as that of training young people to take their places as useful members of a productive workforce.

The corporation's intimate connections with a host of other institutions in modern America were already evident early in the twentieth century. One of the best known of these later in that century was the military-industrial complex, the vast and labyrinthine system tying the military to the industries associated with complex technologies and science. In both America and Europe such ties were clearly evident even before

World War I greatly accelerated the process. For example, "in the closing decades of the nineteenth century," Thomas Hughes pointed out in *American Genesis* (1989), "a naval armaments race gathered momentum and stimulated the ... growth of a military-industrial complex." Hughes noted that the military's support was critical to the beginnings of such early "large-scale technological systems as wireless telegraphy and telephony (radio), the airplane, and feedback guidance-and-control systems for ships and airplanes."

The presence of the corporation was felt even in the heart of the older, agrarian America. The arrival of the railroad in rural communities, mechanization of the farm via the distribution networks of the McCormick Reaper Company and International Harvester, the penetration of agrarian homes by Sears and Montgomery Ward, and the work of agricultural experimental stations all brought the presence of big business firmly into the heartland. Rural cooperatives did their best to imitate the methods of the new organizations in agribusiness, without yielding (at least at first) to the strong profit orientation of those enterprises. Agrarian civilization in turn had its effects on the corporation in the countryside, as Olivier Zunz points out in his "On the Farm" chapter in *Making America Corporate*. Nevertheless it was the values, the technologies, and the ways of the corporation that ultimately would prove the strongest influence on the future of rural life. As the twentieth century progressed, farm life as a whole would be revolutionized by the impact of the corporation's tractors, autos, electric power, and communications systems. The lure of industrial jobs and urban life, along with the declining need for farm labor as a result of mechanization and ever larger farms, accelerated the long-term decline in the farming population.

It also seemed reasonably clear by the early 1920s that the corporations would prove triumphant over their archenemies, the labor unions. Most of the early big businesses in industry managed to keep unions out through a variety of strategies such as the introduction of new production technologies, the use of political influence, high wages, good benefits and other kinds of welfare work, and a willingness to exploit working class ethnic and racial divisions. At the end of the nineteenth century the emergence of the American Federation of Labor as the nation's dominant and defining union organization, the House of Labor, showed that unionism in the United States most often meant craft unions. Under the leadership of the cigarmakers' Samuel Gompers, the AFL unions soon came to abandon political militancy and to focus on economic gains within the system, a pattern ironically called "business unionism." By and large, the AFL's members belonged to unions that found life in the older and often declining sectors of the economy such as the construction trades, mining, and the industries still dependent on skilled craft work (such as Gompers's old cigarmakers' union). As David Montgomery argued in *The Fall of the House of Labor*, "by the end of the depression of 1920–2, American workers' militancy had been deflated, trade unionism largely excluded from larger corporate enterprises, and the left wing of the workers' movement isolated from effective mass influence." Later in the twentieth century the presence and power of unions would wax and then wane under the pressures of the Great Depression, the intervention of the state on labor's side in the New Deal, and the long decline of labor organizations after World War II, but those events lie well outside the bounds of this study.

The new, corporate civilization that had emerged by the first part of the twentieth century was sharply highlighted in the brilliant study in cultural anthropology done by Robert S. and Helen Merrell Lynd and published as *Middletown: A Study in American Culture* (1929). The Lynds and their field staff conducted intensive investigations in 1924–25 in Muncie, Indiana, the community they would call Middletown in their book. Their goal was to compare life as it had been lived in the 1880s to the way it was lived in the mid-1920s, and their work has held up well. They focused on activities such as getting a living, making a home, training the young, leisure, religious practices, and community activities. Their portrait of Middletown illustrated the vast transformation that had swept over the nation since big business arose in industry and brought with it the range of changes discussed above.

The Lynds' major finding was that the meaning of life in Middletown in 1924 was dominated by "getting a living." "The money medium of exchange and the cluster of activities associated with its acquisition drastically condition the other activities of the people," they concluded. Society had come to be divided into two groups, which the Lynds designated the "working class and business class." The two groups kept different hours, went to different churches ("Holy Roller or Presbyterian") belonged to different clubs, and drove different cars (Fords or Buicks). But despite these differences, both groups gave their primary allegiance to the getting of "the money medium of exchange." They found the business class somewhat more satisfied than were the working class with their work and the higher prestige it afforded in the community, but "for very many" in both groups "the amount of robust satisfaction they derive from the actual performance of their specific jobs seems, at best, to be slight." Labor Day had declined from its high place in the 1890s, unions played a much less important role as providers of social functions, and "public opinion is no longer with organized labor."

Since psychological satisfaction was now found less often on the job, more and more people focused on leisure, home, and community activities in search of meaning in their lives. Material progress was in fact providing much more in the way of leisure time and the other good things that could be bought, from household appliances to autos and countless other goods and services. "For both working and business class no other accompaniment of getting a living approaches in importance the money received for their work." The consumer society had come to offer what meaning life afforded for most. "The rise of large-scale advertising, popular magazines, movies, radio, and other channels of increased cultural diffusion from without" the Lynds wrote, "are rapidly changing habits of thought as to what things are essential to living and multiplying optional occasions for spending money." This was the answer to the question posed in *Middletown*'s seventh chapter, "Why do they work so hard?"

For many critics of modern life, this was a deplorable, even a calamitous, outcome. Some have blamed big business for engendering such a materialistic, unrewarding, and alienating society. David Noble's 1977 work, *America by Design,* for example, was a thoughtful and forcefully argued critique of corporate civilization and its alliance with the institutions of technology and science. "Modern Americans," in Noble's view, "confront a world in which everything changes, yet nothing moves. The perpetual rush to novelty that characterizes the modern marketplace, with its escalating promise of technological transcendence, is matched by the persistence of preformed patterns of life which promise merely more of the same." The result, he argued, is "a remarkably dynamic society that goes nowhere." Though they were careful to strike a tone of scientific objectivity in *Middletown*, the Lynds clearly shared many of those same concerns. So have many thoughtful critics of modern life.

Whether there were (and are) meaningful and realistic alternatives to a materialist-based civilization in the United States is a difficult question. From at least the time of the Great Awakening in the middle of the eighteenth century, reformers have preached to the American people about the emptiness of materialism and have sought to lift their vision to some higher plane. On the whole these efforts have thus far fallen on deaf ears.

Certainly the modern corporation was not the root cause of Americans' devotion to materialism. Big business arose, as we have seen, not merely because evil and clever robber barons pulled the wool over our eyes. Nor did it flourish without arousing doubt, criticism, and opposition. The political worries about the dangers posed by big business led to a new level of economic activism by government, though that brought a somewhat muddled and often contradictory set of results. The modern corporation very quickly became the dominant institutional form in American life, forging deep and complex ties with other institutions such as those of engineering and science, education, the military, the polity, and even the older, agrarian ones. The corporations' ways, methods, technological systems, and core values soon affected almost every aspect of daily life in the twentieth-century United States. Perhaps that is what President Calvin Coolidge meant by his famous and cryptic remark that the business of America is business.

Big business arose and triumphed because it was the most effective instrument yet devised to organize and coordinate productive economic activities in a nation where material progress was the purpose of life. Once the transportation and communications networks of the nineteenth century were put in place, it was possible and profitable to build industrial businesses that occupied many sites, carried out many functions, and served many markets. The productive potential of new technologies and of scientific research could then be fully unleashed, and for the first time it became possible to produce more than the economy could absorb. Ironically, at the time when humankind could at last see the way to provide material goods in abundance, society faced another sort of difficulty altogether. The potential for instability and ruin through overproduction, price wars, and boom-and-bust was soon clear to manufacturers and to many others as well. Efforts to master those problems while retaining the productive potential of science and technology were a central part of the overall economic quest in America analyzed by Robert Wiebe in his influential book, *The Search for Order, 1877–1920* (1967).

Through the two paths we traced earlier, vertical and horizontal integration, business leaders in the United States created a new organizational form, one that had not existed at the close of the Civil War outside a handful of major railroads. A few examples appeared in industry in the 1880s and early 1890s. Legal changes encouraged centralized firms, and important shifts in the financial system facilitated mergers. The depression of the 1890s put renewed pressure on prices and greatly speeded the formation of large firms, particularly in the newer industries employing mass production, capital-intensive technologies. By the end of the Great Merger Wave in 1905, big business was in place. Within another decade or so, it was clear how deeply big business would affect labor-management relations, the institutions of government, science and technology, the university, and the military, as well as the daily lives of millions of ordinary Americans, as the *Middletown* study would dramatically underscore.

Those who deplored society's acceptance of big business, its values and its practices, reflected genuine and deeply felt doubts and fears. The subsequent history of American economic growth and the continuing triumph of materialism, however, has shown what the vast majority of Americans seem to want. Certainly it is not all they want, but it is what they want most. Nor is this a peculiarity of the United States. Big business arose in a roughly similar form in Western Europe, with some differences in timing and particulars. Certainly there remained notable national differences in the styles of large-scale enterprise, such as the distinctions Alfred Chandler drew in *Scale and Scope* between America's managerial capitalism, Britain's personal capitalism, and Germany's cooperative capitalism. Even more marked differences were visible in the later rise of big business in Asia. Still, the similarities in the form, function, and activities of big businesses around the world seem more important than the differences. Because the modern corporation has proved to be the most effective means yet created for addressing the remarkably widespread conviction that economic growth and material progress are the *raison d'être* of modern societies, it has emerged as a most powerful element in much of contemporary civilization. Despite deep doubts of the sort voiced by Americans earlier, and despite recurrent ominous signs that uncontrolled economic growth imperils the planet's ecosystems, the lure of industrial capitalism seems ever stronger.

And so it appeared to historian Henry Adams in *The Education of Henry Adams* as he reflected on the triumph of industrial civilization when he visited the great World's Fairs at Chicago (1893), Paris (1900), and St. Louis (1904). Such grand international expositions were popular showcases for the world's cultures and products throughout the last half of the nineteenth century, and Adams was among the many millions who saw and marveled at them. The fairs were also stages for the emerging great corporations, such as the Pennsylvania Railroad, General Electric, Siemens, Westinghouse, and Krupp, which placed exhibitions at many of the expositions that followed the pioneering great World's Fair, London's Crystal Palace Exhibition of 1851. At the Paris Exposition of 1900 Adams observed "the complexities of the new Daimler motor, and of the automobile, which, since 1893, had become a nightmare at a hundred kilometres an hour." What moved him most, however, was "the great hall of dynamos," the generators of the wondrous new energy form of the age, electricity. For Adams the dynamo "became a symbol of infinity, . . . a moral force." "The planet itself," wrote Adams, "seemed less impressive, in its old-fashioned, deliberate, annual or daily revolution, than this huge wheel, revolving within an arm's length at some vertiginous speed, and barely murmuring— scarcely humming an audible warning to stand a hair's breadth further for respect of power—while it would not wake the baby lying close against its frame. Before the end, one began to pray to it." Here the capitalistic, centralizing, and mechanical civilization of the West raised a monument to its new gods— science and technology, organization, and the corporation.

For Henry Adams, the history of western civilization was divisible into only two eras, which he symbolized through the imagery of the Virgin (or Venus) and the Dynamo. From the beginnings of western civilization, the dominant force was the Virgin—the mystery of fecundity and religion, or what Adams called "love of God and lust for power in a future life." With the coming of the scientific revolution and the rise of technology that began in the Renaissance, however, humankind in the West began to embrace a new, secular faith. Materialism, the machine, and finally the corporation brought the triumph of that new faith in the forces he saw embodied in the Dynamo. And "the Trusts and the Corporations," he gloomily concluded in his autobiography, "stood for the larger part of the new power that had been created since 1840. . . . They were revolutionary, troubling all the old conventions and values, as the screws of ocean steamers must trouble a school of herring." The corporation had emerged as the most highly perfected institution of a civilization that worshipped the force of the Dynamo. It still is.

As we struggle with the problems and the dangers that accompany the corporate cornucopia, we will likely do so with the methods, institutions, and habits of mind that have shaped our industrial, corporate civilization. We have cast our lot with the corporation, the engineer, and the scientist. Together we have made a material, technical world, as Adams sensed while standing before the dynamo in Paris, on the cusp between the nineteenth and the twentieth centuries. To break out of this world would require that we adopt fundamentally new values, as Adams believed the western world had done by gradually but decisively shifting its allegiance from the Virgin to the Dynamo. Such changes are possible, but they do not happen easily, and they do not happen often.

BIBLIOGRAPHICAL ESSAY

Although historians and many others in America have long agreed that business has played a central role in the history of the United States, its place in the study of American history has never been central. Throughout most of the period during which professional historians have sought to understand and explain their country's history, the focus was on the political events and personalities of the past. The colonizing of the eastern coast by Europeans, the struggle for political and cultural independence from Great Britain, the rise and evolution of political parties, the expansion of the physical boundaries of the country and the settlement of those new areas by European immigrants, the conflicts between the various regions or sections of the nation, and the country's diplomatic affairs and its wars—these were what American history was all about. The focus was primarily political, and on the whole the actors in the story were eminent, white, and male (or Great White Men, as later critics put it). In part because of the powerful impact of the work of the historian Frederick Jackson Turner emphasizing the influence of the frontier in shaping America, many came to feel that the United States was distinctive, indeed almost unique, as compared to the history of the European nations. The common experience of conquering a continent and building a civilization from the wilderness, many historians argued, helped to make the United States much more egalitarian, democratic, and open than the European societies from which it sprang. Business was seen as having played only an incidental role in the story.

Because most historians traditionally conceptualized the American past as a struggle for ever more democratic political forms and the extension of economic opportunity to more and more citizens, they tended to view business as a negative, excessively conservative force. But, except for occasional episodes such as the struggle over the nature of the banking system in the early decades of the nineteenth century, business was seldom seen as being central to the American story. That changed with the rise of big business. Once large-scale enterprises appeared in the economy, they began to attract both political attention and increasing notice, and criticism, from historians.

Our perspective on the rise of big business has undergone a number of shifts since Americans first began to think and write about these giant institutions. From the initial appearance of large-scale firms until the decade of the 1970s, most of the public and much of the scholarly discourse about their role focused on the question of how to discipline and control such powerful private interests in a democratic society. Americans worried and argued about robber barons and antitrust. All the while, big business developed into the most dominant, influential institution in our society.

In the era following World War II, the modern corporation, along with the United States military, became the most important vehicle through which American influence was projected around the globe. Among professional historians, the prevailing analytical framework came to be the "consensus" school. Powerfully influenced by the experience of World War II and by the climate of the Cold War, historians emphasized another variant of the idea of American uniqueness. Building on the insights of Alexis de Tocqueville's *Democracy in America*, scholars such as Louis Hartz, Richard Hofstadter, and Daniel Boorstin argued that the United States had on the whole been "born free" of the European conflicts over class and property. Because Americans never had to undergo the crisis of a struggle to displace an established aristocracy based on birth and never had any truly serious disagreements over the desirability of private property and competition, the United States was thought to have enjoyed a remarkably wide consensus over fundamental political and economic issues. The basic purpose of the society was to be the pursuit of material growth, its fundamental decision-making process was to be democratic, and there was to be a relatively high degree of freedom of individual political expression. Within that wide and deep consensus there had been many struggles, of course, but the conflicts were over less basic questions than the ones that divided European countries that had fought bloody revolutions to uproot privileged aristocracies and had remained locked in the mid-twentieth century in a grim struggle over whether capitalism or communism would ultimately define their societies.

Despite the broad agreement on the desirability of private property and capitalism, however, business continued to be seen by American historians as a negative, threatening force, with the business community acting primarily as a brake slowing the long-term progress toward a more nearly equal and free society. Business was regarded as perhaps the closest thing in the American past to the evil tradition of aristocratic privilege in Europe. Big business was seen as a persistent threat because of its great power and influence in American society, especially in the political system. The corporation was a dangerous beast that had to be tamed or caged by the countervailing political power of liberal, left-oriented political movements such as those of the Progressives and Franklin D. Roosevelt's New Deal in the 1930s. The apparatus of regulation and the antitrust laws (put in place beginning in the 1880s) and the welfare state of the 1930s represented political efforts to discipline large-scale business enterprise and to soften the harsher edges of an individualistic, sharply competitive economic system.

In the 1960s Americans experienced another powerful wave of concern about the abuse of private economic power. This produced the scholarship of the New Left, manifested in such works as Gabriel Kolko's harsh indictment of the liberal tradition and its view of progressivism, *The Triumph of Conservatism* (1963). Criticism from the left crested at a time when the American corporation was reaching its zenith in the markets of the world. Indeed, so strong did U.S. business seem to the rest of the world that one of the era's most popular issues abroad was how to respond to what many saw as the dangerous growth of American economic and cultural imperialism. One of the era's most popular and influential books, Jean-Jacques Servan-Schreiber's *The American Challenge* (1968), voiced Europeans' deep anxieties about the spread of American business overseas. At home Americans both loved and feared the corporation, but few at that time regarded it as weak or incompetent.

As the relative power of the United States waned during and after the 1970s, Americans came to see big business in a rather different light. Not only had it become an accepted part of the cultural landscape, it now seemed less threatening. More and more, the leading political question about business came to be, not how to contain an expanding corporate sector, but how to restore it to its former health. Inevitably, this has affected the way in which scholars think about the history of big business. Some seek explanations of more recent weakness and competitive decline in the era when American business was still gaining strength, but that projects too many of the concerns of the present into the past and distorts history. Without going that far, it is nevertheless possible to see that the recent relative decline of American business has altered and in some ways sharpened our understanding of the rise of big business.

As in so many other aspects of national life, Americans have become much more sensitive to the international context in which the modern corporation arose in the United States. Although America led the way in the creation of big business and its dominance of contemporary industrial and postindustrial society, other nations clearly experienced many of the same developments, though in somewhat different patterns and often at later points in time. One of the effects of the heightened perception of these similarities was to erode further the belief in America's uniqueness, which contributed to the decline of the consensus school of American historiography. In addition, the social conflicts of the 1960s and the increasing tendency of historians to analyze history with regard to particular sectors of society (especially women, racial and ethnic minorities, and ordinary Americans) rather than to attempt to interpret the history of the society as a whole made it increasingly difficult to understand the American past from any overarching point of view.

Historians' heightened sensitivity to the worldwide context of the history of the United States in general and of modern business enterprise in particular has been evident in the work of the scholar whose writings now dominate the study of large-scale business, Alfred D. Chandler, Jr. Chandler's *Strategy and Structure* (1962) and *The Visible Hand: The Managerial Revolution in American Business* (1977) established the framework in which most scholars now understand the history of big business, and both studies focused almost exclusively on developments in the U.S. and the activities of U.S. enterprises abroad. Thereafter, Chandler's interests broadened to include more of the international context. His *Scale and Scope* (1990) addressed the similarities and the differences among the histories of the modern corporation in various nations around the world, particularly those in the United States, Great Britain, and Germany.

Chandler's early work signaled the decline in scholarly interest in the "robber barons or industrial statesmen" approach to the topic. The first historical "school" dealing with the rise of big business (and one that still dominates popular versions of the history of this topic) was formed by the writers emphasizing the immoral and socially irresponsible role of the "robber barons." Charles Francis Adams, Jr. and his brother Henry set the tone for much later writing in their assessment of the shady hijinks of early American railroad moguls, *Chapters of Erie* (1886). The brothers Adams blended revulsion with perhaps a pinch of secret admiration, and their lively treatment is still highly readable today. Henry Demarest Lloyd's *Wealth Against Commonwealth* (1896) was an early assault on one of the nation's most closely studied corporations, Standard Oil (now Exxon). Lloyd's perspective was that of what might be termed "Christian socialism," and many other historians of this school have shared a similar inclination. A bible for such interpretations was Gustavus Myer's three-volume *History of the Great American Fortunes* (1907–1910), which attacked the methods by which prominent business leaders had acquired their great wealth. After a decline during World War I and the inhospitable 1920s, this critical interpretation was revived during the Great Depression. Matthew Josephson published what became the standard work of this school, *The Robber Barons: The Great American Capitalists, 1861–1901* (1934). In Josephson's view, a handful of business pirates unscrupulously fought their way to controlling much of the nation's economy, and (as he argued four years later in *The Politicos*) of the nation's political apparatus as well. This way of looking at the history of business proved remarkably resilient, particularly in the general textbooks of American history and in American history survey classes. It even had some influence in the way those in other nations regard the United States, as demonstrated by such studies as Marianne Debouzy's *Le Capitalisme "Sauvage" aux Etats-Unis, 1860–1900* (1972).

During the 1940s and 1950s, the opposing view was represented by the school known as the "industrial statesman" historians. Writing at the time of America's and American business's dominance of the postwar world, these scholars emphasized the heroic achievements of the generation of business leaders who built big businesses. They pointed to the efficiency of rationalized competition and its role in expanded economic growth. Then too, the Cold War had its effect. The postwar era was one in which many people thought of economic growth as a weapon in the global conflict with communism (the clearest sign of that was the wide influence of cold warrior Walt Rostow's *The Stages of Economic Growth: A Non-Communist Manifesto,* 1960). Historians who emphasized the positive achievements of big businesses almost always saw those accomplishments in significant measure as personal triumphs, the work of extraordinary individuals. Most of the "industrial statesmen" group, in fact, were biographers. Such laudatory works as Allan Nevins's *John D. Rockefeller: The Heroic Age of American Enterprise* (1941), Ralph and Muriel Hidy's *Pioneering in Big Business, 1882–1911* (1955), also about Rockefeller and his associates, and Julius Grodinsky's *Jay Gould* (1957) reinforced the idea that big business was the work of a generation of men of uncommon ability. Relatively little attention was given to trying to understand and explain patterns in the evolution of large corporations. Politics and personalities continued to comprise the lens through which the rise of big business was usually viewed.

Other approaches to the history of American business did emerge, but they captured the imagination neither of general historians nor of the broad public as did the good-versus-evil pairing of "robber barons or industrial statesmen." For example, Thomas C. Cochran tried over a long and distinguished career to direct historians' attention to the social context and consequences of business's influence in American life. Cochran produced an extensive, excellent body of studies from the 1940s into the 1970s that analyzed the interaction between the institution of business and other institutions in society, including religion and education. Perhaps the book that best summarized Cochran's ideas and his sociological approach to history was his *Business in American Life: A History* (1972). Although many American historians would follow Cochran's lead into social history from the 1960s on, his work led to the founding of no "school" of business history.

Business historians also found little of interest in the approach of the so-called "New Economic History" that utilized economic theory and statistical analysis. That new approach certainly swept the field of economic history in the United

States, as is apparent in the contents of the Economic History Association's *Journal of Economic History* from the early 1960s on. Methodological disagreements and unfamiliar sets of questions kept business historians from seeing very much of real use in the New Economic History. In the United States, the study of business has remained more the work of persons trained in university departments of history rather than in departments of economics, and many historians have resisted the theoretical and econometric approach. Louis Galambos's quantitative content analysis study, *The Public Image of Big Business, 1880–1940* (1975) was an exception, and so was the work of his student, Naomi Lamoreaux, as in her impressive study, *The Great Merger Movement in American Business, 1895–1904* (1985). On the whole, however, historians of business have made only limited use of economic theory in attacking questions about business enterprise in the American past.

The work that did shape the field of business history in a fundamental way was, of course, that of Alfred Chandler. This has been true not only for the study of business history in the United States, but throughout the world. No other historian has ever exercised such a strong influence over the study of business history as has Chandler. Virtually every work now written on the history of modern, large-scale enterprise must begin by placing itself within the Chandlerian analytical framework. Over the course of more than three decades, Chandler's prodigious and highly focused scholarship yielded a body of work that virtually *became* business history. He directed his great energies at essentially a single set of interrelated questions. Like Ahab pursuing the White Whale, Chandler tenaciously pursued the large corporation. He sought to answer these questions: When, where, and why did it arise? How did it persist? Where did it spread? How was it organized? What functions did it perform? So influential was this approach that it almost crowded out other questions and methodologies. It reinforced the already strong tendency for historians to think of the history of business as the history of big business only, and to ask first how any firm's or industry's past fit into the structuralist-functionalist or strategic-structural framework. (For a summary of Chandler's ideas, see Thomas K. McCraw, ed., *The Essential Alfred Chandler: Essays toward a Historical Theory of Big Business*, 1988.)

Chandler's approach proved influential among a wide circle of historians and others in disciplines such as business administration. (It was my privilege to be Chandler's student, and his work has strongly influenced this book.) Indeed, there grew up over time a related set of historical studies that collectively represent what Louis Galambos has termed the "organizational synthesis." Galambos summed up his ideas on this body of historiography in two influential essays in the *Business History Review*, "The Emerging Organizational Synthesis in Modern American History" (1970), and an update, "Technology, Political Economy, and Professionalization: Central Themes of the Organizational Synthesis" (1983). This interpretive framework, Galambos wrote in the second of those essays, emphasized "organization building, both public and private, and the creation of new and elaborate networks of formal, hierarchical structures of authority that gradually came to dominate our economy, polity, and culture."

This trend in time carried historians' interests outside the "internalist" focus of Alfred Chandler's work. In particular, topics in labor history, the history of work, of government's and women's roles in the economy, and above all, the history of technology have expanded our view of the meaning of big business's growth. The interdisciplinary work of Philip Scranton (*Proprietary Capitalism*, 1983, and *Figured Tapestry*, 1989) reminded us that much of American history in the last century involved industries that did not fit the dominant paradigm of big business and mass production. Still, it is those topics that remain at the heart of the "organizational synthesis."

Since big business arose primarily as a means of creating, expanding, and controlling an increasingly technical economy and society, it was natural that great attention should be paid to the history of modern technology. The work of Lewis Mumford, especially his *Technics and Civilization* (1934), gave structure to the topic and did much to launch the discipline of the history of technology. Siegfried Giedion's *Mechanization Takes Command* (1948) gave a broad and rich account of the coming of the machine age and was a pioneering study in the history of everyday life. More recently the major work was that of Thomas P. Hughes, who has highlighted and analyzed the role of invention, the rise of complex technical systems, technological momentum, and the broad cultural impact of modern technology. Beginning with his biography of *Elmer Sperry: Inventor and Engineer* (1971), Hughes crafted a remarkable body of scholarship. His *Networks of Power: Electrification in Western Society, 1880–1930* (1983) broke new ground in the transnational, comparative study of scientific and technical systems that are interwoven with both economics and politics. Although he explicitly denies that complex technical systems are autonomous, Hughes's work nevertheless argues that "it is difficult to change the direction of large electric power systems—and perhaps that of large sociotechnical systems in general." Like Chandler's, Hughes's work causes the reader to consider the possibility that technological determinism shapes history, though both take pains to disassociate themselves from that suggestion. With *American Genesis* (1989) Hughes offered a new synthesis emphasizing the central role of inventors, industrial scientists, engineers, and designers in the making of America after 1870. He also described the influence of American models on the European modernists of the twentieth century, such as the Bauhaus group and Le Corbusier.

The vital role of science-based, high-technology industries in modern economies has drawn the attention of many other historians of technology besides Thomas Hughes. Hugh G. J. Aitken's two books on radio (*Syntony and Spark—The Origins of Radio,* 1976, and *The Continuous Wave,* 1985) traced the subtle interactions among science, technology, and the marketplace. The history of research and development in the modern corporation was analyzed in many studies, including Reese V. Jenkins, *Images and Enterprise: Technology and the American Photographic Industry* (1975), George Wise, *Willis R. Whitney, General Electric, and the Origins of U.S. Industrial Research* (1985), Leonard S. Reich, *The Making of American Industrial Research: Science and Business at GE and Bell, 1876–1926* (1985), and David A. Hounshell and John Kenley Smith, Jr., *Science and Corporate Strategy: Du Pont R&D, 1902–1980* (1988). All gave clear evidence of the intimate connections between the modern corporations in science-based industries and the institutions of science and technology, including the universities. David Noble's *America by Design: Science, Technology, and the Rise of Corporate Capitalism* (1977) presented a sharply critical account of the nexus among business, engineers, and scientists in the twentieth century. Other important contributions from historians of technology included David A. Hounshell, *From the American System to Mass Production, 1800–1932: The Development of Manufacturing Technology in the United States* (1984), which analyzed a major strain in the history of mass production from the federal armories of the early republic through the automobile industry. Much remains to be explored on the historical ground where the military, business, and technology met, but important contributions are to be found in the chapter entitled "Brain Mill for the Military" in Thomas Hughes's *American Genesis: A Century of Invention and Technological Enthusiasm, 1870–1970* and the essays in Merritt Roe Smith, ed., *Military Enterprise and Technological Change: Perspectives on the American Experience* (1985).

The literature on other topics tied to the rise of big business—Taylorism, work, and the changing nature of the workforce and labor-management relations—is vast. The body of work dealing with unions and strikes is even more vast, though the role of unions in industries dominated by big business was not great in the era prior to the New Deal. There is room here to mention only a few sources. Joseph Litterer's 1963 article in the *Business History Review*, "Systematic Management: Design for Organizational Recoupling in American Manufacturing Firms," is the beginning point in any study of systematic management. Frederick W. Taylor and his followers have been the subjects of many articles and books. Hugh G. J. Aitken's *Taylorism at Watertown Arsenal* (1960) was an early case study that remains highly useful. An unusual and notable biography of Taylor done from a psychological point of view was Sudhir Kakar, *Frederick Taylor: A Study in Personality and Innovation* (1970). An invaluable account of the rise of the engineering profession, the engineer's relation to business, and the ideology of engineering was contributed by Edwin T. Layton, Jr, in his oddly titled book, *The Revolt of the Engineers: Social Responsibility and the American Engineering Profession* (1971). Layton focused on the conflicts between the demands of business and the engineering profession's ethical demands; most readers will conclude that the engineers did not revolt but instead soft-pedaled their commitment to social responsibility. Daniel Nelson's *Managers and Workers: Origins of the New Factory System in the United States, 1880–1920* (1975) was a balanced and thorough treatment of the technological, managerial, and personnel changes that affected the workplace in the period covered in this book. David Montgomery's *The Fall of the House of Labor: The Workplace, the State, and American Labor Activism, 1865–1925* (1987) is a rich, wide-ranging look at the struggles over control of the shop floor, the new management systems and styles, the political milieu, and the battles between unions and management that left the AFL in a rigid and weakened condition by the beginning of the 1920s. Montgomery's study looks backward into the nineteenth century, while Sanford M. Jacoby's *Employing Bureaucracy: Managers, Unions, and the Transformation of Work in American Industry, 1900–1945* (1985) looks forward from the turn of the century events toward the mid-twentieth-century state of labor and management. Jacoby's work is particularly strong on the topic of the creation of modern personnel practices and the workings of labor "markets" inside the corporation.

Life inside the corporation is the focus of a growing body of literature that continues to move beyond an interest in the political context and the conflicts between unions and management. JoAnne Yates's *Control through Communication: The Rise of System in American Management* (1989) was a good example of this, demonstrating in tangible detail the ways in which modern organizations were able to record, transmit, summarize, and communicate data and decisions throughout highly complex bureaucracies. Alongside works such as that of Sanford Jacoby, mentioned above, Yates's in-depth look at the inner workings of bureaucracy gives us an even better understanding of the day-to-day functions of big business.

The task of fitting big business into the surrounding social and cultural context is one that still calls for more attention. Again, the work of Lewis Mumford and Siegfried Giedion are essential beginning points, along with Reyner Banham's *Theory and Design in the First Machine Age* (1960) and *A Concrete Atlantis: U.S. Industrial Building and European Modern Architecture, 1900–1925* (1986). Thomas Hughes's contributions on the cultural impact of mechanization, design, and architecture in industry were a further reminder of the riches that can be mined by historians exploring the interconnections between big business, technology, and the social matrix from which they sprang. Similarly exciting was the work of Olivier Zunz in *Making America Corporate, 1870–1920* (1990). By examining the creation of what the Lynds called the "business class" in *Middletown*, Zunz opened exciting frontiers that are in some ways similar to those initially explored by Thomas Cochran in his long and much-honored career. Much more attention in the future seems likely to be given to the consequences of big business on American culture, now that Alfred Chandler has given us such a solid understanding of the evolution of the modern corporation as an organizational form.

And it is clear that the topic of the political implications of the rise of big business can never be exhausted. That, as we have seen, was the first focus of historians' interest in the appearance and consequences of the modern corporation and concentration in industry. Thomas K. McCraw's thoughtful and gracefully written *Prophets of Regulation* (1984) was a reminder of the unanswered questions that remain concerning just how people learned to live with and shape the behavior of the enormous corporations that dominate modern life in the United States as well as in much of the rest of the world. Louis Galambos and Joseph Pratt, *The Rise of the Corporate Commonwealth: U.S. Business and Public Policy in the Twentieth Century* (1988) pointed to the criticisms of "the inflexibility and inefficiency of American business and political institutions" that began in the 1970s, reviewed the history of such institutions since the days of J. P. Morgan, and argued that the system is still strong and capable of responding to its difficulties.

The economic, technological, and social triumph of big business and its subsequent increasingly global scope have done much to homogenize our world. Even the nation state itself has become less powerful as many decisions of global impact are taken in the headquarters of international corporations and not in the halls of government. The highly visible economic success of the modern industrial enterprise, whether in the United States, Germany, Britain, Sweden, Japan, or Singapore, has flowed from and reinforced an apparent notion that the purpose of life is material gain. Much, indeed most, of the world's population has yet to enjoy the fruits of industrial progress, and as more populations do so, ecological and demographic problems will surely multiply. As societies and scholars struggle to understand these cultural transformations, they will do so with the benefit of a reasonably coherent historical picture of the emergence of big business, industrial capitalism, and industrial society. It was the great contribution of Alfred Chandler and the analysts of the organizational synthesis that gave us a new understanding of the dynamics of the most revolutionary institution of our age. In time, of course, this historical understanding will wear thin and be replaced by other questions and new perspectives. Just as no single strategy or structure, whatever its value, is permanently successful in the world economy, no set of historical ideas can stand indefinitely. Interest in the rise of big business, however, seems likely to endure.

INDEX

The Rise of Big Business, 1860–1920, Second Edition was copyedited, proofread, and managed through production by Lucy Herz. Maureen Hewitt was sponsoring editor. The text was typeset by Impressions, a division of Edwards Bros. Inc., and printed and bound by McNaughton and Gunn, Inc.

The cover and text were designed by Roger Eggers.